Multinational
Computer Nets

Multinational Computer Nets

The Case of International Banking

Richard H. Veith
Logica Inc.

LexingtonBooks
D.C. Heath and Company
Lexington, Massachusetts
Toronto

Library of Congress Cataloging in Publication Data

Veith, Richard.
   Multinational computer nets.

   Bibliography: p.
   Includes index.
   1. Banks and banking, International—Data Processing. 2. Computer
networks. 3. Interorganizational relations. I. Title.
HG1709.V4   332.1'5'02854   80-8386
ISBN 0-669-04092-4   ✓

Published simultaneously in Canada

Printed in the United States of America

International Standard Book Number: 0-669-04092-4

Library of Congress Catalog Card Number: 80-8386

Contents

List of Figures
and Tables

Acknowledgments

Professor Evelyn Daniel of Syracuse University deserves considerable thanks for her direction and suggestions while I was conducting the research for this book in the university's School of Information Studies. Other faculty who also deserve thanks for their time and insights are Professor Edwin Bock, Professor Jeffrey Katzer, and Dean Robert S. Taylor of Syracuse University and Dr. Oswald H. Ganley, then temporarily at Harvard University and a member of the U.S. State Department. The research was partially supported by funds from the Syracuse University Office of Research and Graduate Affairs.

I would also like to thank Rodney E. Buckmaster of Manufacturers Hanover Trust Company, Morris H. Crawford of the U.S. Department of State, John J. Dempsey of Marine Midland Bank, Stephen A. Ernst of the Bank of America, William L. Fishman of the National Telecommunications and Information Administration, Cees J. Hamelink of the Institute for Social Studies at The Hague, Bruce W. Hasenyager of Citibank, Ed Hawley of Wells Fargo Bank, Karen E. Koritz of Information Gatekeepers Inc., William J. LaBelle of Security Pacific National Bank, John A. Lengyel of Mellon Bank, Andrew Lloyd of the *Transnational Data Report*, Eiichi Matsumoto of the Bank of Tokyo, Eric O'Brien of SWIFT, J.J.N. Rost Onnes of Algemene Bank Nederland, Steven Rubin of Wells Fargo Bank, and Frank J. Yautz of Westdeutsche Landesbank Girozentrale for providing information and answering questions.

Finally, I am extremely grateful to the anonymous bank officials who responded to my several sets of questionnaires and especially to those officials who took the time to add additional notes and commentary.

Introduction

Information is instrumental in social organization. Lately, the abilities to store, duplicate, and transmit information have increased so dramatically that students of human society have called information a key resource, a fundamental of life so basic as to be ultimately undefinable. Even life itself has been characterized as essentially an information-processing system.[1] Lewis Branscomb, chief scientist at International Business Machines Corporation (IBM), calls information a frontier, which suggests that there is still something unknown, waiting to be conquered.[2] On the other hand, we do know that the development of complex civilization can be linked directly to the building up of repositories of information outside the human brain.[3]

There is no doubt that in the past two decades the storing and transmitting of information has mushroomed. This is largely the result of the merger of energy, materials, and know-how that produced computer/telecommunications systems.[4] Karl Deutsch suggested in 1965 that we were entering a new stage in history, the computer revolution, which would eventually rival the Renaissance.[5] An analysis of the growth of computer systems as well as publications and scientific and technical knowledge itself shows that all are growing exponentially, with an even greater escalation since the mid-1960s.[6] By 1985, according to another estimate, there may be some 175,000 large-scale computer systems in the world, with single databases containing up to 10^{12} bits of information; to put it another way, about 400 of those databases could collectively contain all the information in all the world's libraries.[7] And these estimates do not involve the faster-growing numbers of minicomputers and microcomputers.

It must be pointed out, however, that the development of the computer did not create the exponential growth in the store of recorded information. This had been taking place for several centuries at least. The computer merely happened to be the machine that stepped into a situation of expanding information that already existed. In 1945, Vannevar Bush's vision of a machine to handle the growing mountain of information files was not a computer (although digital computers were being developed during the war) but a desk-sized repository of microfilm that, he suggested, might be designed to accept 5,000 new pages a day for hundreds of years before becoming full.[8]

The Information Economy

At the same time that the growth of recorded information was beginning to be recognized as a possibly explosive phenomenon, it was also suspected that increasingly larger percentages of the population were becoming primarily involved in information production and transmission.

Fritz Machlup is generally considered to be the first researcher in the United States to try to quantify this occupation and preoccupation with information. Thus it might be helpful to take a quick look at how Machlup decided we were approaching an information-oriented society.

In a series of lectures in 1959 and 1960, Fritz Machlup developed the idea of studying what he called "knowledge production," which included information production, since Machlup argued that in everyday usage information and knowledge often refer to roughly the same thing. In 1962 he produced his influential book *Production and Distribution of Knowledge in the United States*, which pulled together population, income, education, and industry statistics from a variety of sources including the U.S. Department of Commerce, the U.S. Department of Labor, the U.S. Department of Health, Education and Welfare, the Internal Revenue Service, the U.S. Office of Education, the National Academy of Sciences, the National Science Foundation, the United Nations *Statistical Yearbook*, and the United Nations *Demographic Yearbook*.[9] Machlup defined knowledge-producing activity to include information gathering and distribution that might be only part of some other major activity. For example, he suggested that 50 percent of a doctor's time can be considered in the knowledge production or dissemination category, since doctors do spend a lot of time giving information.

Machlup's examination of both industries and occupations was divided into five categories of knowledge production: education, research and development, communication media, information machines, and information services. Under the industry approach, Machlup concluded, after extensive qualifications, that total knowledge production in 1958 accounted for almost 29 percent of the gross national product (GNP). From 1954 to 1958 the knowledge-producing industries were growing at a weighted annual rate of 8.8 percent, while the GNP was growing at only 5.1 percent annually. The fastest-growing branch was computers, expanding at a rate of 104 percent per year. Similarly, using the occupation approach, and again with extensive qualifications, Machlup found that knowledge-producing occupations (including students, since they mentally produce knowledge or store information) increased from 13.5 percent of the potential civilian labor force in 1900 to 42.8 percent of the potential labor force in 1959. In terms of growth, this meant that the knowledge-producing occupations grew by 602 percent from 1900 to 1959, while the labor force itself grew by only 131 percent during that same time. Machlup explained that the trend was toward not only more people in knowledge occupations but also people more skilled, since the fastest-growing groups were, first, clerical, then administrative and managerial, and finally, in the late 1950s, professional and technical personnel.

The next major attempt to examine the available statistics in the United

States was undertaken by Marc Porat, building directly on Machlup's work and on the writings of Daniel Bell, Peter Drucker, and others. Porat's purpose was to define an information sector within the U.S. economy from two perspectives: information labor and information capital. Further, he defined a primary information sector, where information goods and services are exchanged in a marketplace, and a secondary information sector, where the information services are for internal consumption by, for example, government and non-information firms.[10]

Porat's conclusions, based primarily on data from the U.S. Bureau of the Census and the U.S. Bureau of Labor Statistics, were that 25.1 percent of the GNP in 1967 originated in the primary information sector and that another 24.1 percent of the GNP originated in the secondary information sector. By Porat's definitions and calculations the work force in the information sector grew from 15 percent in 1910 to over 40 percent in 1970, with information workers reaping 53 percent of all labor income in 1967. Again, some qualifications are in order. Defining what information is and how it is produced colors the results. Porat argues that, since a clock gives information about the time but can also be an ornament or a piece of furniture, the casing portion of the clock can be placed in one category and the clock mechanism itself in another—the latter is information producing but the former is not.

In a recent interview, Porat suggested that his proposal for treating information capital (and labor) as distinct from noninformation capital (and labor) had not yet been accepted as the basis for extensive quantitative research but that when such research is completed it will probably show that certain combinations of information capital and information labor are very productive and other combinations may be definitely unproductive.[11]

This does not mean that Porat's work has been disregarded. The Organization for Economic Cooperation and Development (OECD) is using Porat's model to quantify the information sectors in Austria, Canada, Finland, France, Japan, Sweden, and West Germany, as well as in the United States. Preliminary indications are that all countries show similar increases in the information sectors, although not to the extent found in the United States. Reportedly, information workers in Canada increased in number from 29.4 percent of the work force to 39.9 percent from 1951 to 1971. In Japan, information workers increased from 17.9 percent of the work force to 29.6 percent from 1960 to 1975. And in West Germany the increase was from 18.7 percent to 34.1 percent of the work force from 1950 to 1976.[12] The definition of information and information workers used in the OECD studies is said to be more restrictive than that used by Porat, thus including fewer occupational categories.

All this concern with counting and estimating the size and extent of information gathering, storing, and disseminating is what underlies the popular feeling that ours is an information age and an information economy.

Postindustrial Society

Porat was influenced in his research by, among others, Daniel Bell and his book *The Coming of Post-Industrial Society*. Published in 1973, Bell's thesis is that in thirty to fifty years we will see the emergence of postindustrial society.[13] Bell originally formulated the concept around 1962, using the term *postindustrial* to denote a service society that is no longer primarily concerned with producing goods.

A postindustrial society, says Bell, is characterized by an intellectual "technology" based on information; this so-called intellectual technology arises alongside machine technology. The primary institutions in this society, he explains, will be universities, academies, and research corporations, and the primary resource will be human capital. There is also expected to be more conscious decision making in the activities of the postindustrial society, based on the increasing amount of information available.

According to another viewpoint, there will be a radical increase in the speed and load of communications in the postindustrial society such that people, not markets, will actively determine the allocation of resources—in other words, a trend toward societywide planning.[14]

To some extent, we can already see attempts to plan society on a broad scale. A study called "The Plan for an Information Society" was produced by the Japan Computer Usage Development Institute in 1972, although it is more of an attempt to forecast than an attempt to create or control future social development.[15] The study outlined essentially four stages of the computerization of society, with the last two stages still in the future. The first stage was from 1945 to 1970, during which the dominant use of computers that affected society was their use in large-scale national projects. The second stage began about 1955 and ended in 1980 and was characterized by the use of computerized information systems for more efficient management of organizations. In the third stage, which began about ten years ago and may not end until 1990, information is used broadly in many areas of activity, that is, the computerization is now society-based, and the object of computerization is no longer individual organizations but society as a whole. By the time of the fourth stage, from 1980 to 2000, computerization will be based on the individual person and the general public will have numerous information machines and will possess the ability to use them. The expectation, according to the study, is that in the fourth stage our ability to produce knowledge will grow much more than in the past.

In short, the information age is well on its way, if you accept the definitions of information sectors and information-based intellectual technologies. And part of what is meant by the information age is the effect on organizations, and societies, of the use of large computerized information-processing systems.

International Perspective

Because the computer/telecommunications combination permits relatively easy global access to large stores of information, investigations of the information age soon become international in scope. The OECD has argued that the international dimension is, in fact, indispensable for constructing sound information policy, since human knowledge is a function of humanity as a whole.[16]

As an international organization, the OECD has been concerned with broad information policies for nearly twenty years. The OECD's Information Policy Group was established in 1964, and recommendations for information policy began being published around 1970. For society to fully appreciate and utilize the combination of computer/telecommunications, the OECD called for the recognition of an information infrastructure, that is, a new substructure underlying political, economic, and social structures. National and international policies were recommended to facilitate the introduction and shaping of the new infrastructure. If, instead, the present organizational structures of the computer and telecommunications industries prevail, the OECD reports have said, many of the riches of the combined technologies will be lost.[17]

There continue to be predictions about the impacts and effects of international computer/telecommunications systems. Daniel Bell, in a 1979 article, judges the computer/telecommunications phenomenon to be a fourth revolution in human social history, following the revolutions in information exchange produced by the developments of speech, writing, and printing.[18] Bell writes that the new mix of telecommunications is not only faster but also organized in a totally new way. The result, he goes on, is that personal interaction is increased, the cost of distance is drastically reduced, and the arenas of social interaction are enlarged. An example of the latter result is the genuine international economy that has developed. The crucial issues, says Bell, are access to information and restrictions on information monopolies (with exceptions for systems protecting public health and safety).

A Parallel

Anyone attempting to analyze the impact of computer networks would do well to look at similar studies of the impact of the telephone. In the introduction to *The Social Impact of the Telephone*, the comment is made that while all of the changes of the century may have stemmed from science and technology, still unanswered is the question of just how important was the telephone's specific technology.[19] The social effects of the telephone seem to lie in diverse, often opposing directions: the telephone invades privacy and yet protects privacy; the telephone permits dispersed coordinated activity and, at the same time, tight central control; the telephone makes information exchange possible over great distance without loss of time but helps lose information by sidestepping writing; the telephone helped create congested city centers and helped extend the suburbs. And yet the telephone, without a doubt, say the book's authors, adds to human freedom. It is a liberating device permitting effective action in many directions.

The social effects of computer networks may ultimately be as diverse (if not more so) as those of the telephone, since they are now intertwined technologies. Perhaps by addressing the phenomenon in its first ten or twenty years, instead of waiting a hundred years as seems to have been the case with the telephone, a little more understanding of the social impact of the technology may be gained. There is little doubt that social impact of some sort is, and will be, occurring.

Notes

1. See, for example, Lila L. Gatlin, *Information Theory and the Living System* (New York: Columbia University Press, 1972), p. 1.

2. Lewis Branscomb, "Information: The Ultimate Frontier," *Science* 203 (January 1979): 143.

3. L.B. Heilprin, "On the Information Problem Ahead," *American Documentation* 12 (January 1961): 6.

4. The combination of energy, material, and know-how is a concept suggested by Kenneth Boulding, "The Future of the Interaction of Knowledge, Energy and Materials," *Behavior Science Research* 13 (1978): 175.

5. Karl Deutsch, "Knowledge in the Growth of Civilization: A Cybernetic Approach to the History of Human Thought," in *The Foundations of Access to Knowledge*, ed. Edward B. Montgomery (Syracuse, N.Y.: Syracuse University Press, 1968), p. 54.

6. Georges Anderla, *Information in 1985* (Paris: Organization for Economic Cooperation and Development, 1973), pp. 28-33.

7. Ibid.

8. Vannevar Bush, "As We May Think," *Atlantic Monthly* (July 1945): 106.

9. Fritz Machlup, *Production and Distribution of Knowledge in the United States* (Princeton, N.J.: Princeton University Press, 1962).

10. Marc U. Porat, *The Information Economy: Definition and Measurement*, 9 vols. (Washington, D.C.: U.S. Government Printing Office, 1977).

11. "Porat Urges More Research," *Information World*, March 1979, pp.1, 18.

12. "Information Sector Growth," *Information World,* March 1979, p. 17.

13. Daniel Bell, *The Coming of Post-Industrial Society* (New York: Basic Books, 1973).

14. Leon N. Lindberg, "Strategies and Priorities for Comparative Research," in *Politics and the Future of Industrial Society,* ed. Leon N. Lindberg (New York: David McKay, 1976).

15. See Yoneji Masuda, "Privacy in the Future Information Society," *Computer Networks* 3 (June 1979): 164-170.

16. Organization for Economic Cooperation and Development, *Information for a Changing Society* (Paris: Organization for Economic Cooperation and Development, 1971), p. 19.

17. "The Use of Computers and Telecommunications: Towards an International Policy," *OECD Observer,* February 1973, p. 17.

18. Daniel Bell, "Communications Technology—For Better or for Worse," *Harvard Business Review* 57 (May-June 1979): 20-42.

19. Ithiel de Sola Pool, ed., *The Social Impact of the Telephone* (Cambridge, Mass.: MIT Press, 1977), pp. 5-9.

Multinational
Computer Nets

1 Interorganization Relations

Research in interorganization relations is based on the assumption that broad social and environmental aspects must be considered, especially with an appreciation of history. Howard Aldrich prefaces his *Organizations and Environments* with the remark that analyzing changes in organizational forms requires knowledge of historical trends in political, economic, and legal systems, including international patterns.[1] Along the same lines, interorganization researchers have been urged to relate their work to the larger problems of postindustrial society.[2] Interorganization research seems well suited, then, as an approach for analyzing one of the major technological developments of the past twenty years, namely, the construction of international computerized information processing networks.

The goal of this book is to gain an understanding of what has happened: this book describes and explains the interorganization relations in a given industry with particular emphasis on information sharing and exchange via computer/telecommunications networks. Moreover, the interorganization relations approach will be used to place this analysis within the larger social and political environment that has developed over time.

The first half of this book describes and discusses interorganization research, multinational data traffic, and computer networks in international banking, and the second half of the book presents and analyzes some current data on interbank relationships, suggesting some patterns. Specifically, the rest of chapter 1 will summarize interorganization research and the variables that have been used and the role of computer/telecommunications networks in the interorganization relations. Chapter 2 sets the study within the larger context of the transborder data flow debates, which have encouraged studies of network use and have resulted in various forecasts of political, economic, and social effects. The debates over transborder data flow have taken place within and among at least a dozen or so international bodies and have accompanied the enactment of data laws in nearly a dozen countries. In chapter 3, justification is presented for choosing international banking, giving a preliminary account of the extent of information networks in banking, and presenting structural effects that have been suggested in the literature. It is worth noting that banking has been recognized as a prime segment of the information economy.[3]

Chapter 4 contains current data on aspects of telecommunications-based relationships in international banking. The data were gathered in a survey of the largest commercial banks in the world. The 140 participants in the survey represent eleven countries and about fifty institutions. The fifth chapter uses techniques of interorganization-relations research to place the development of computer/telecommunications in international banking within a broader, more historical context. And the sixth and final chapter summarizes the research, looks at implications, and suggests areas for further work.

Before discussing the research trends in interorganization relations, however, it might be helpful to review one of the first studies that addressed the question of the social impact of using computer networks that cross national borders. In 1972, the Center for Futures Research at the University of Southern California undertook a Delphi study of the social implications of using computers internationally.[4] The authors of the research felt that the international aspect, by itself, changed everything. The social and organizational ramifications would be quite apart from those associated with networks at the domestic level. Approximately sixty prominent experts in computers and telecommunications, from government, industry, and academics, were surveyed using the Delphi technique of recirculating forecasts so that the participants could take others' views into account if desired. The broad questions behind the survey concerned the probable impact on governments, the probable impact on corporations, and the expected effects on individuals and entire societies.

Generally, the participants predicted more homogeneity and increased fear of the mechanization of life. Although opinions covered the full scale, most of the participants agreed that global data banks would gradually homogenize the way people understand and interpret problems and would result in a uniform body of information used in doing so. Three-fourths of the participants also thought that the international computer networks would contribute to a blending of cultural tastes and attitudes. Regarding fear of mechanization, 84 percent of the participants agreed that multinational computer systems would increase the level of fear some people feel in connection with computers, yet 72 percent also thought that inability to interact effectively with computers would be a crippling form of illiteracy.

The Delphi panel saw primarily legal and political barriers to the development of the multinational information systems. For example, the lack of a legal process for solving questions of control and liability for the multinational use and storage of data was selected as one of the most important possible barriers to the utilization of the information systems. Other barriers strongly agreed on were the clashing of political views and the tension between socialism and capitalism, the divergence of laws regarding business practices, and concern for military security.

Regarding the projected increase in the use of multinational information systems by corporations, the participants generally agreed (and sometimes quite strongly) that the systems would permit greater integration of a corporation's activities, would increase professionalization of management (that is, use of the systems would require more management education), and would enhance the power and influence of multinational corporations. The forecasters disagreed, however, by four to one, with the notion that highly centralized, hierarchical management structures would result. Instead, the computer networks might have a tendency to decentralize management by making more information available to the branch offices. The participants saw only slight, if any, movement in the direction of uniformity of relevant national laws. This latter result tends to support the decentralization forecasts, since some from of decentralized activity might be required simply to operate within the bounds of the laws of given countries.

For less developed nations, the multinational computer networks were not seen as particularly beneficial economically. Although the use of such networks might accelerate industrialization, the gaps between rich and poor countries would not be magically bridged, and a form of "information dependency" might develop. On the other hand, perhaps over a longer period of time, the experts thought that multinational computer networks would provide opportunities for developing nations to improve administration in such areas as planning, finance, and statistics and that information networks would enhance technology transfer and the integration of the developing countries into the world economy.

The survey's authors concluded that many of the major impacts would be felt within ten years (by 1982 or 1983), and that multinational computer/ telecommunications systems may be one of the three or four most important factors in bringing nations closer together. Raymond Vernon, in his study of multinational corporations and an interdependent world economy, supports this conclusion, stating that during this century technological forces have pushed nation-states together, specifically mentioning telecommunications and computers as well as commercial aviation.[5]

This larger question of the social impact of using transnational information systems underlies the present study also. To attempt at least a partial answer, attention will be directed to those interorganization relations (in international banking) that are based on transnational computer/telecommunications networks.

Organizations and Systems

The study of interorganization relations is grounded in organization theory and definitions of organizations and systems. It is not always easy to say just what is or is not an organization. March and Simon, in *Organizations*, refuse to define the term, saying more or less that you know one when you see one.[6] Another text explains, at first, that organizations are human collectivities existing as such for the purpose of achieving some goal and then goes on to offer a more detailed definition of the collectivity that includes the notions of boundaries, authority, communication, continuity, and, usually, goals.[7] Robert Presthus, who summarizes organization theorists from Weber to Simon, adds that most organizations have characteristics such as hierarchy, status anxiety, considerable size, rationality, and "efficiency."[8] Presthus put quotes around efficiency because, he argued, efficiency in organizations is almost impossible to demonstrate or maintain.

One of the first characteristics that must be dealt with is the reasonably recognizable boundary. If you draw the boundary large enough, the question arises as to whether you have enscribed an organization or a larger social system. Barnard, for one, points out that organizations operate within larger social systems.[9] Price's *Handbook of Organizational Measurement* follows a common trend in saying that organizations are a subset of social systems and gives the examples of families, peer groups, and communities as social systems that are not organizations.[10] Price's definition, as he notes, comes from the Talcott Parsons-Amitai Etzioni tradition of defining organizations. Katz and Kahn directly address the problem of locating an organization's boundaries by introducing open-system theory into the definition of organization. An organization is described as an energic input-output system, an open system drawing in energy through transactions between the organization and its environment.[11] Traditionally, then, setting the bounds of organizations has not been an easy task. As will be seen later, this problem persists in defining a coherent group or set of interorganization relations.

A second characteristic of organizations is that they are often believed to have goals in mind. It is generally stated that organizations exist to accomplish some specific goals. However, Presthus, for example, does not mention organizational goals explicitly, and Katz and Kahn take issue with the whole idea of describing an organization as a group means for accomplishing some stated purpose. Katz and Kahn feel that organizations commonly do not do what they were explicitly designed to do and that it is best to start with concepts that do not require the identification of the purposes supposedly in the minds of organization planners. Nevertheless, Katz and Kahn's input-output model seems to accept common goals as a part of the definition of organizations, since product or purpose is included as part of what makes an organization. Presthus too cannot ignore the fact that organizations have at least limited objectives. Thus the presence of some common goal or set of goals seems to be a key aspect of organizations. This is also posited to be true for a group or cluster of organizations with substantial interorganization relations.

To move from the level of individual organizations to organized groups, we find some similarities. And international banking, as an entity, seems at first glance to fit the definition of an organization, especially Chester Barnard's description of the beginnings of an organization as a group of people who are able to communicate and willing to contribute action for a common purpose.[12]

The common purpose can be the desire, within limits, to stabilize the world economy (whether this is so will be dealt with in the later chapters). Even granting some limited common purpose, problems appear if we begin to search for other characteristics of traditional organizations, such as ranks of authority. On the other hand, if we turn to definitions of future organizations (which will be discussed later), international banking does seem to fit the model. The benefit of recognizing this, if it is accurate, is that it answers part of the question of the social impact of transborder data flows, and it allows organization theories, such as theories of decision making and problem solving, to be applied to this larger grouping.

In interorganizational studies, there have been a number of phrases used to refer to the joint, coordinated action of organizations, for example, joint decision making, concerted decision making, interorganization relations, interorganization system, interdependence, and organization-set.[13] The latter phrase refers to a systems model suggested by Evan, in which an organization or class of organizations is the focus, and, using role-set analysis, the interaction of the focal organization with its environment is studied.[14] None of the phrases, however, captures the organizationlike relations that seem to be forming among multiorganization clusters using high-speed computer/telecommunications. Thus it might be more useful to use the term *cluster organization* for this purpose.

This term was in fact suggested by Thomas Whisler to refer to business organizations of the future.[15] The key to the cluster organization is the computerized information system. Whisler suggests that a cluster organization would exhibit diversity in location, output, structure, and internal advancement for employees. An earlier book by Whisler stressed the same theme, that is, that in the future businesses would appear to be more loosely organized but would be held together by computer/telecommunications technology.[16] The technology would facilitate international operations and conglomerate mergers but would probably not do away with hierarchy entirely. In yet another publication, Whisler suggested that a cluster organization is one in which there is a high degree of cooperation among specialists, with a computer as the central core.[17] He then went on to say that perhaps the military would be an example of just such an organization.

Although Whisler was talking about individual organizations, the phrase seems readily applicable to the close grouping of firms sharing communication channels and information databases and working together for a common purpose. Ramström, in his outline of the future organization in "Toward the Information-Saturated Society," provides further details of what might be a cluster organization.[18] His characteristics of future organizations are: arrangements for processing and transmitting information among relatively independent units; coordination among the units on a fairly direct basis; no clear unity of command; no clear organizational levels; multiauthority relationships; a central pool of planners coexisting with relatively independent divisions; and a favoring of decentralization.

The cluster organization of banking appears to match all the requirements of the organization of the future: information processing networks (for example, an international network, and use of the same databases); relatively independent units (the different banks); close working relationships (correspondent relationships, joint networks, and, for example, syndicated loans); central planning (the central banks); a lack of unity of command and no clear hierarchical structure (the banks of one country or even within any country are not hierarchically above other banks); multiauthoritarian relationships that are harmonized (the national laws affecting bank-data transmission); and a trend toward decentralization.

This, then, is the point of the study: to what extent can we say that computer/telecommunications networks have facilitated the emergence of cluster organizations? To answer that, techniques of interorganization-relations research will be used to probe relations in international banking.

Interorganizational Research

The study of interorganization relations, which has been developing over the past ten or fifteen years, has produced a number of different approaches and a handful of dimensions or variables that have won general agreement.

Marrett summarized five principal approaches to interorganization relations research in an attempt to bring together a number of converging interest areas and to establish some common terminology.[19] According to her classification, the first approach concentrates on the intraorganization aspects, such as complexity, norms, and openness of communication. The second approach is comparative, looking at similarities of goals and structures and compatibility of philosophies. The third approach addresses relations, that is, the network is the unit of study and the variables are, for example, reciprocity, cooperation, intensity of the relations. In the fourth approach, attention is given to contextual properties such as the history of interlocking relations and Evan's organization-set. The final approach complements the previous approach by looking at nonorganized contexts such as economic conditions and community support. (Naturally, these approaches are found in various combinations in the literature.) Marrett then proposed four major variables of interorganization relations research: formalization; intensity; reciprocity; and standardization. (See table 1-1.) These variables will be discussed further in chapter 4 in relation to the survey results presented in that chapter.

Not all investigations of interorganization relations have used the four dimensions summarized by Marrett. Another researcher, Benson, explained in 1975 that there was still conceptual confusion and overlap in the study of

Table 1-1
Dimensions of Interorganization Relations

Major Dimension	Component Variable
Degree of formalization	Agreement formalization
	Structural formalization
Degree of intensity	Size of investment
	Frequency of interaction
Degree of reciprocity	Resource reciprocity
	Definitional reciprocity
Degree of standardization	Unit standardization
	Procedural standardization

Source: Based on Marrett, "On the Specification of Interorganizational Dimensions," *Sociology and Social Research* 56 (October 1971): 83-99.

interorganization relations, adding that the interorganization network is an emerging phenomenon.[20] He proposed to unify the theoretical work with four concepts: domain consensus, ideological consensus, positive evaluation, and work coordination. However, Benson's intent was only to produce concepts useful in studying social service agencies, and, as he admitted, the analysis of the relations among business organizations is beyond his scheme.

One of the avenues of inquiry that comes up repeatedly in interorganizational studies is that of interlocking directorates. Mariolis analyzed the directorships of 797 of the largest U.S. corporations in 1970 (500 industrials, 50 banks, 50 insurance companies, 50 retailers, 50 utilities, and 47 others) and found that interlocking was all-pervasive.[21] Of the total number of corporations, 736 had at least one interlock, and a link could be traced directly through 722 of them. The average corporation was only four steps from about 92 percent of all the other corporations.

Mariolis' study is particularly of interest because he examined banks specifically, testing the theory that corporate control in the United States is centered in banks. Of the 21 most interlocked corporations, 10 were banks or bank holding companies. (See table 1-2.) But, because of the pervasiveness of interlocks, being a bank was only modestly associated with interlocking. Thus Mariolis concluded that although banks were indeed heavily interlocked, the evidence for bank control was unclear, since interlocking directorates do not necessarily mean control and may even be structurally irrelevant. He did say, though, that banks help to integrate the economy.

Another approach to studying interorganization relations is to view the relations as a means of reducing uncertainty in the environment. Pfeffer and Salancik discuss a number of ways organizations have worked together for

Table 1-2
Interlocking Directorates among Banks

Bank Company	Number of Interlocks[a]
Chemical New York Corporation	82
First National City Corporation	72
Chase Manhattan Corporation	62
J.P. Morgan	60
First Chicago Corporation	68
National City Bank of Cleveland	57
Mellon National Bank and Trust	51
Bankers Trust New York Corporation	46
Continental Illinois	46
Harris Trust and Savings Bank	45

Source: Based on Peter Mariolis, "Interlocking Directorates and Control of Corporations: The Theory of Bank Control," *Social Science Quarterly* 56 (December 1975): 425-439.

[a]The median number of interlocks for Mariolis's 797 corporations was 8.

that reason, for example, in trade associations, cartels, reciprocal trade agreements, coordinating councils, advising boards, boards of directors, and joint ventures.[22] Pfeffer and Salancik suggest that the net result of interorganization relations seems to be the creation of larger organizations existing in environments that are increasingly regulated and politically controlled. They also feel that the trend is, or will be, in the direction of more concentration of power and decision making and away from decentralization.

The assumption that interorganization relations serve a useful purpose, namely, as a way to control an uncertain environment, has been called into question, at least in part, by Whetten and Leung.[23] Some relationships may continue to exist even after a useful purpose has been served, or the relationships may have been initiated for reasons unrelated to achieving control over the environment. In fact, Whetten and Leung point out that relationships may be perceived as liabilities rather than assets. Further, they maintain, little research has focused on the dysfunctional consequences of interorganization links, particularly loss of autonomy.

Social network analysis has also been applied to the study of interorganization relations, even though social network analysis is usually employed for interpersonal relationships. Stern summarizes the work done by Benson, Aldrich, and others in social network analysis and concludes that the methodology is often allowed to dominate the substantive theoretical questions and that the quantitative cross-sectional approach of network analysis fails to recognize the importance of the historical development of interorganization relations.[24] Stern's position is that social network analysis must be supplemented by examining the environmental context, interaction processes, history, and the specific nature of the network under study. In his examination of intercollegiate athletics (the NCAA), Stern found that the four structural determinants or variables suggested by Benson and Aldrich (namely, administrative structure, degree of system coupling, multiplexity of ties, and new network resources) were not enough to explain the development of the network and the decision by the member organizations to surrender authority to the NCAA. The examination of the determinants alone missed the process; the decision to allow the NCAA to become a powerful control body (in 1952) was a complex interaction of environment, structure, and process.

Macrostructure

The research into interorganization relations has come from, and subsequently contributed to, broader studies of political and economic systems or, as some have phrased it, the macrostructure. It is impossible to summarize or even mention all the theorists, researchers, historians, and writers who have contributed to this area, but it is probably helpful to at least indicate that the connections are there.

One of the works often mentioned in interorganization literature is C. Wright Mills's *The Power Elite*.[25] Mills's position is that the means of information and power are centralized and that a few persons' decisions come to affect the great majority of the "ordinary" people. But Mills does not say that the powerful elite are engaged in conspiracy or even in unified action. Instead he simply points out that there are psychological and social reasons for unity and increasingly more compelling reasons for working together. To put it another way, coordinated action seems to be the easiest way of accomplishing goals on a large scale.

In direct opposition to Mills is Alain Touraine, who sees no cohesive group of power elite.[26] However, Touraine's thesis does lead him in the direction of the cluster organization to the extent that, in the evolution of business organizations, the individual organization begins to fill a subordinate role in a larger system. The efficiency of the firm comes to rely more and more on social and political factors. And, according to Touraine, international financial and industrial groups may be working out the economic policy that affects any individual business. John Kenneth Galbraith seems to be saying much the same thing when he posits that the "technostructure" has the same survival goals as any organization.[27]

Galbraith also says that industrial systems are converging and that they are converging with the state. But another eminent scholar, Arnold Toynbee, does not see such easy convergence in the near future (although Toynbee may agree with Galbraith in the very long term). Instead, Toynbee feels that global economic life and the political organizations of the world's nations are drifting farther apart.[28] The rise of interdependent or unified political systems has often followed far behind interdependent economic systems. Toynbee notes that the Roman Empire was an economic unit at least four centuries before it was a political unit. The one institution, or set of organizations, he says, that is currently the bridge between political systems and the world economy is the multinational corporation.

Role of Computer/Telecommunications

Although many studies and theories of interorganization relations and the macrostructure acknowledge the role of technology, the necessity of the technology is often understated. The rise of the transnational cluster organization would not have been possible without the presence of international telecommunications facilities and data networks, whatever other preconditions may also have been necessary. Raymond Vernon writes that multinational corporations in general are striking examples of the extent to which telecommunications networks permit integrated organizations to be geographically dispersed.[29] As early as 1936, Luther Gulick wrote that the problem of organization is one of an effective network of communication and control, and, looking at the new developments of television and two-way radio, he went on to say that such developments brought entirely new possibilities to organization.[30]

It is not simply the communications facilities that have brought new possibilities for organizing but the advent of computer networks and information processing as well. Herbert Simon has stated that it is obvious that without communication there can be no organization and that decision making—one of the primary principles of organization—often hinges on the transmission of information.[31] It should be just as obvious that present day multinational organizations would not be the same without the current telecommunications and computer networks.

The Cluster Organization

The real social impact of the computer/telecommunications network, however, is not so much in permitting traditional organizations to expand geographically as in permitting newer forms of organization, such as the cluster organization. Some implications of this are that the cluster organization works together for a common purpose and that the firm's own boundaries mean less than the functioning of the cluster organization as a whole.

The cluster organization concept, as presented here, is in short a bringing together of ideas from a number of disciplines, a synthesizing of definitions and descriptions provided by social and organizational researchers. The cluster organization is technologically possible because of the greatly increased speed, volume, and accessibility of information in computerized information processing networks. Concurrent with the technical developments have been a series of psychological and social (including political and economic) changes that utilize the technology. Together, these have encouraged or produced the cluster organization, that is, an organization that is: based on computerized information networks; composed of semiindependent units; marked by a lack of hierarchical structure at the top and by multiauthority relationships; and influenced by central planners coexisting with the independent divisions.

The key aspect, arising from the question of the social impact of transborder data flows, is the shared computerized information processing networks. This is what distinguishes the cluster organization from cooperatives and associations, which have formed the basis of interorganizational relations studies in the past. Some of the research suggests that member organizations may gradually give up some power and control to a central organization, becoming less and less defined as the larger organization (with still the traditional characteristics of hierarchy of authority) gains more power. But the theory of the cluster organization does not suggest that. Facilitated by high-volume, high-speed, easily accessible channels of information flow, the cluster organization of the future may be able to exist as an organization without a clear hierarchy of authority and consisting of relatively independent units, yet still adhering to common goals.

To summarize, this book uses the techniques of interorganization relations research (primarily the dimensions first outlined by Marrett) to analyze transborder data flow in a specific industry, namely, international banking. In this way, it may be possible to see some specific contributions of computer/telecommunications in interorganization relations and the degree to which a set of relationships can be called a cluster organization.

Notes

1. Howard Aldrich, *Organizations and Environments* (Englewood Cliffs, N.J.: Prentice-Hall, 1979).

2. J. Kenneth Benson, "The Interorganizational Network as a Political Economy," *Administrative Science Quarterly* 20 (June 1975): 229-249.

3. Marc U. Porat, "Defining an Information Sector in the U.S. Economy," *Information Reports and Bibliographies* 5 (May 1975): 23. See also, Philip H. Abelson and Allen L. Hammond, "The Electronics Revolution," *Science* 195 (18 March 1977): 1087-1092.

4. Burt Nanus, Michael Wooton, and Harold Borko, "The Social Implications of the Use of Computers across National Boundaries," *AFIPS Conference Proceedings 1973* (Montvale, N.J.: AFIPS Press, 1973), pp. 735-745.

5. Raymond Vernon, *Storm over the Multinationals* (Cambridge, Mass.: Harvard University Press, 1977).

6. James G. March and Herbert A. Simon, *Organizations* (New York: John Wiley and Sons, 1958).

7. Richard H. Hall, *Organizations: Structure and Process* (Englewood Cliffs, N.J.: Prentice-Hall, 1977), pp. 22-23.

8. Robert Presthus, *The Organizational Society* (New York: St. Martin's Press, 1978), p. 19.

9. Chester Barnard, *The Functions of the Executive* (Cambridge, Mass.: Harvard University Press, 1956), p. 82.

10. James L. Price, *Handbook of Organizational Measurement* (Lexington, Mass.: Lexington Books, D.C. Heath, 1972), p. 2.

11. Daniel Katz and Robert L. Kahn, *The Social Psychology of Organizations* (New York: John Wiley and Sons, 1966), pp. 14-18.

12. Chester Barnard, *The Functions of the Executive* (Cambridge, Mass.: Harvard University Press, 1956), p. 82.

13. See, for example, the collection of papers in Matthew Tuite, Roger Chisholm, and Michael Radnor, eds., *Interorganizational Decision Making* (Chicago: Aldine, 1972).

14. William M. Evan, "An Organization-Set Model of Interorganizational Relations," in *Interorganizational Decision Making*, ed. M. Tuite et al. (Chicago: Aldine, 1972), pp. 181-200.

15. Thomas L. Whisler, "The Business Organization of the Future," in *Organizations of the Future*, ed. Harold Leavitt et al. (New York: Praeger, 1974), p. 187.

16. Thomas L. Whisler, *Information Technology and Organizational Change* (Belmont, Calif.: Wadsworth, 1970), pp. 115-117.

17. Thomas L. Whisler, *The Impact of Computers on Organizations* (New York: Praeger, 1970), p. 154.

18. Dick Ramström, "Toward the Information Saturated Society," in *Organizations of the Future*, ed. Harold Leavitt et al. (New York: Praeger, 1974), pp. 174-175.

19. Cora Bagley Marrett, "On the Specification of Interorganizational Dimensions," *Sociology and Social Research* 56 (October 1971): 83-99.

20. J. Kenneth Benson, "The Interorganizational Network as a Political Economy," *Administrative Science Quarterly* 20 (June 1975): 229-249.

21. Peter Mariolis, "Interlocking Directorates and Control of Corporations: The Theory of Bank Control," *Social Science Quarterly* 56 (December 1975): 425-439.

22. Jeffrey Pfeffer and Gerald R. Salancik, *The External Control of Organizations* (New York: Harper and Row, 1978).

23. David A. Whetten and Thomas K. Leung, "The Instrumental Value of Interorganizational Relations: Antecedents and Consequences of Linkage Formation," *Academy of Management Journal* 22 (June 1979): 325-344.

24. Robert N. Stern, "The Development of an Interorganizational Control Network: The Case of Intercollegiate Athletics," *Administrative Science Quarterly* 24 (June 1979): 242-266.

25. C. Wright Mills, *The Power Elite* (New York: Oxford University Press, 1959).

26. Alain Touraine, *The Post-Industrial Society* (New York: Random House, 1971).

27. John Kenneth Galbraith, *The New Industrial State* (Boston: Houghton Mifflin, 1971).

28. "Arnold Toynbee: Are Businessmen Creating the Pax Romana?" (interview) *Forbes,* 15 April 1974, pp. 68-70.

29. See James H. Sood, "Personal Privacy: Can the MNCs Afford to Respect It?" *Columbia Journal of World Business* 14 (Spring 1979): 42-51.

30. Luther Gulick, "Notes on the Theory of Organization," in *Papers on the Science of Administration*, ed. L. Gulick and L. Urwick (New York: Columbia University Press, 1937), pp. 1-46.

31. Herbert A. Simon, *Administrative Behavior* (New York: Macmillan, 1961, p. 154.

2 The Transborder Data Flow Debates

At least six international groups have been working during the past decade or so to bring about mutually beneficial procedures for interconnection of computer networks. Despite the competition and conflict that mark international politics and economics, there has been continual concerted effort by groups such as the Organization for Economic Cooperation and Development (OECD) and the Council of Europe in the area of transborder data flow that has resulted in similar policies and laws in a number of different countries, especially in Western Europe. This chapter outlines some of the international effort at harmonization and concludes with a discussion of the types of issues raised in the data-flow debates, suggesting that there is a broad underlying desire for truly international and mutually beneficial solutions.

Background

The roots of telecommunications, computers, and information systems have been traced back centuries and even millenia across many cultures. However, the international use of computer/telecommunications networks did not begin until the 1950s with the establishment of airline and defense networks. According to a brief article in the *Times* (London), the first public demonstration of an international data communications system was in 1963, when a terminal in England was used to control a computer at the Honeywell plant in Massachusetts, with the control signals being sent via a standard telex line.[1] By way of reference, the first telephone cable across the Atlantic had only been installed a decade earlier, in 1955-1956, although permanent telegraph cable service across the Atlantic had been available since 1866. On the other hand, a mere two years after that demonstration, in 1965, the first commercial communications satellite service was in operation.

By the middle of the 1960s, the computer/telecommunications combination was accepted as the way of the future. By 1965, in the United States, remote access to informational databases was already the case to some extent in the areas of hotel and airline reservations, stock market quotations, banking, insurance, timesharing services, and of course military command and control systems.[2] As the quantity of data traffic grew during the 1960s, the major problems or issues were recognized as economic and political rather than technical. A survey of the regulatory situation in the United States in 1967 described a confusing, complex array of American Telephone & Telegraph (AT&T) tariffs lacking Federal Communications Commission approval, conflicts with state regulatory agencies, who often lacked technical expertise, and nonstandard offerings by various operating companies within the Bell Telephone System.[3]

The regulatory situation in the United States then settled down somewhat, but internationally the complexity and confusion remain, as sovereign states try to solve their interconnection problems beset by political and economic forces. Yet there has also been intense effort at international consensus regarding the development of multinational computer networks, at least among some sets of countries.

International Efforts

OECD

The OECD was established in 1960 and is composed of twenty-four member nations including Australia, Canada, Japan, New Zealand, Turkey, and the United States, as well as countries of Western Europe. Predecesor organizations to the OECD had been working on information policies since about 1950, and the Information Policy Group was created within the OECD in 1964. In 1969, the Computer Utilization Group of the OECD's Directorate for Scientific Affairs took particular notice of possibilities for multination computer systems, commissioning a series of reports on computers and telecommunications and related government policies. Some of these reports have been published as volumes in the OECD Informatics Studies. By 1971, OECD influence was related to a growing recognition among government leaders in the industrial countries of computers and information processing networks.[4] The term *transborder data flow* was apparently used for the first time in international debate during an OECD seminar in 1974.

One of the OECD informatics publications, a report of a 1975 conference, contains a series of papers and studies from a number of countries, including background reports by Ithiel de Sola Pool and Edwin Parker of the United States. Pool's paper detailed the growth of telecommunications facilities, concluding that information technologies will facilitate cultural diversity—unlike mass media's tendency to impose a singleness of style—and that concerns over computer/telecommunication's threats to national sovereignty were misguided and misplaced.[5] The Parker paper, written with Marc Porat, urged intellectual analysis in place of technology forecasting and outlined arguments for an information economy. The paper proposed that, on a global scale, everyone could conceivably win in the game of information processing.[6] The conference concluded that, although information resource management might yield substantial benefits, there were dangers as well, and present-day developed countries might wind up as economic backwaters. The future discussion of international information systems was expected to center on legal questions (such as personal privacy and proprietary business data) and economic obstacles (such as protecting business interests, strengthening domestic information-processing services, and muting the effects of foreign data processing).[7]

An OECD symposium on transborder data flow and the protection of privacy was held in Vienna in 1977 to assess the privacy laws in thirteen nations that could affect international information traffic. Nearly three hundred participants took part in the conference; their collective conclusion was that with regard to networks and information technologies, national issues are closely related to international issues, that legal aspects must be considered in conjunction with the inseparable economic and political aspects, and that various national laws must be internationally coordinated and harmonized.[8]

By early 1978, a new high-level Expert Group on Transborder Data Barriers headed by the chairman of the Australian Law Reform Commission had been established to draft basic guidelines for transborder data traffic and the protection of personal information. At the same time, the OECD continued to work closely with other international organizations, such as the Council of Europe, to foster a more homogeneous environment in international data regulation.

In 1980, the OECD prepared a draft treaty for data protection and privacy and sent the treaty to the OECD's Council of Ministers, where considerable delay was expected.[9] Some member countries asked for more time to evaluate the subject and may seek amendments requiring equivalent national laws as a precondition for treaty compliance. Previously the OECD had recognized the likelihood of delay and had urged that during the interim period no adverse action be taken by any individual member country regarding transborder data traffic.[10]

One of the major attempts by the OECD to ascertain the current status of transborder data traffic was a study sponsored by France, West Germany, the Netherlands, Norway, Spain, and Sweden, and undertaken by Logica Ltd., a London computer and telecommunications research and consulting firm. The final report, *The Usage of International Data Networks in Europe*, is a survey of twenty-three private (leased-line) networks used by multinational corporations and international organizations, and of six data networks operated by public telecommunications authorities.[11] Table 2-1 lists the types of organizations surveyed and rough estimates of the annual volume on most of the networks. The survey sought to determine why organizations engage in transborder data traffic, how the networks developed, how the networks are used, what security restrictions are employed, and the costs and economics of the networks.

In general, the survey reported, organizations use leased-line networks for the following reasons: to coordinate production and marketing, to

Table 2-1
Private Leased-Line Data Networks in the OECD Survey

Organization	Number of Countries[a]	Rough Estimate of Annual Volume (billions of characters)
SITA (airlines)	32	38[b]
SWIFT (banks)	17	10
Oil company	17	15
Industrial manufacturer	17	12
WMO (weather)	12	0.5
Oil company	10	–
Computer bureau	7	1.8
Computer bureau	7	–
Computer bureau	5	72
Computer bureau	5	14.7
Computer bureau	5	11.4
Holiday organization	6	3
Oil company	4	1
Industrial manufacturer	3	0.5
Credit authorization	3	–
Computer bureau	3	1
Clearing bank	2	1.5
IIASA (research)	2	1.2

Source: Compiled from *The Usage of International Data Networks in Europe* (Paris: Organization for Economic Cooperation and Development, 1979).

[a]Where computers or terminals are located, linked by leased line. Does not include dial-up access.

[b]Estimate is for computer data (Type A), does not include an additional 65 billion characters of messaged-switched teleprinter data (Type B).

coordinate financial management, to share data-processing resources, to reduce the cost of telephone circuits; to share scientific and technical research; to improve accuracy and security of information transfer (e.g., by using standard message formats and data encryption techniques); and because the nature of the business might demand international data exchange (for example, airline reservation systems, international banking and credit, and world weather monitoring). The study narrowed down the many applications to eight types: (1) production and distribution; (2) financial management; (3) personnel and payroll (found to be only a minor application); (4) banking and credit control; (5) use by government and public authorities (for example, for statistical work and simulation studies); (6) scientific and technical research; and (8) environmental monitoring.

The security measures employed by the networks, such as authorization codes and data encryption, were judged to be well suited to the applications, with quite strong security measures protecting the banking networks and some applications on the timesharing networks.

The leased-line networks developed largely because the public switched telephone networks are not suitable for reliable high-speed data traffic, and users have relatively little control over access times and data security. Once organizations underwent the expense of leasing lines, they then developed techniques and hardware, such as multiplexors and concentrators, to gain the maximum use for their money.

The study lists twenty-seven separate conclusions, among them the following:

Substantial financial benefits have accrued because resources are used more efficiently.

Some companies have changed their operations drastically to take advantage of the networks.

Use of the networks stimulates international cooperation.

International interdependence has increased but at the same time the risks have decreased because operations can be moved relatively easily from one processing center to another.

International agreements are needed to facilitate the beneficial uses of the networks.

International data transmission, the study says, is already very important, if not essential, to large organizations, but the full potential, of course, is still in the future.

Council of Europe

The Council of Europe, established in 1949 and composed of twenty member nations, formally initiated a study in 1968 of the extent to which the European Human Rights Convention of 1950 contained sufficient safeguards for protecting individuals from any harmful effects of modern technology. The Council of Europe's Committee of Ministers was also charged with the task of examining the laws of member countries for similar safeguards. A group of human-rights experts conducted the survey and reported back to the Committee of Ministers in 1970 that the laws had not in fact kept pace with the technology, especially with computer technology, although the experts also thought that on the whole computers seemed to offer better safeguards than manual systems for the protection of sensitive information.[12]

The key issue in the report to the ministers was the argument that people should always have legal means for discovering what information about them was on file in a computer database. A task force was then requested, in 1971, to produce recommendations for suitable legislation to protect such access. Two years later, the Committee of Ministers was presented with a resolution for data protection in the private sector and in 1974 with a similar resolution affecting the public sector. The Council of Europe adopted the resolutions and urged the member countries to adhere to the principles articulated, although no new laws were actually suggested. However, several national laws were in fact being considered, and in some cases enacted, during those years. An analysis commissioned by the Council of Europe in 1975 showed that the European countries concerned with data protection had indeed followed rather closely the principles of the Council's resolutions.

The Council of Europe has been similarly active in seeking distinctly international law covering the transborder transmission of data. In 1972, several models of a proposed international agreement were presented to the Council, including, for example, a Danish model and a French model. After four years of consideration, the Committee of Ministers asked the Data Protection Committee to prepare an international convention or treaty to supplement the various existing national laws and to provide a unified procedure for solving data flow problems. The intent of the new convention is to eliminate any barriers to transborder data flow that might arise from reliance on strictly national laws.

According to Frits Hondius, one of the leading Council of Europe officials involved in transborder data issues, the draft convention contains solutions to the problem of balancing freedom of information rights with privacy rights in the area of data processing and computer storage.[13] Hondius maintains that both Western Europe and North America share the same basic philosophy in these matters, with the only major differences in implementation being: (1) the European countries prefer omnibus laws rather than sector laws, (2) the European laws are designed to cover more rights than simple privacy rights, and (3) Europeans believe a supervisory authority is necessary to protect the individual.

Although the convention or treaty is initially being prepared to cover only Western Europe, observers from Australia, Canada, Japan, and the United States have been participating. The Council of Europe's Committee on Legal Affairs was to consider the convention or treaty in mid-1980; if approved, and subsequently accepted by the Committee of Ministers, the convention will probably face the ratification process sometime after 1981.

European Community

The European Community (which joins the European Atomic Energy Commission, the European Economic Community, and the European Coal and

Steel Commission, and dates back to the Treaty of Rome of 1957) sponsored a report in 1973 that urged a European-based computer manufacturing industry and at the same time took note of internationally linked computer databases. Regarding the latter, the report called for political consensus on the matter because it affected constitutional rights.[14] There was also an economic concern, as the European Community noted that almost 90 percent of the value of the computer equipment market came from firms with their decision-making centers outside Europe.[15]

The privacy of personal information in databases was addressed by the European Parliament, a division of the European Community, in 1974. The next year a resolution was adopted urging a Community directive to protect individual rights and to avoid the rise of conflicting national laws.

During 1976 and 1977, the Community's civil service, the Commission, produced a summary and analysis of relevant privacy or data protection laws, bills, or proposed legislation in member countries. A subcommittee of the Parliament's Legal Affairs Committee was also active, among other things holding public hearings on minimum standards for data protection, and discussing legal foundations for Community action and possible methods for Europewide data protection. As a whole, the European Community has also begun a systematic examination of database systems and software and their uses. This research is being done under contract by an international joint effort of the National Computing Centre (in the United Kingdom), Gesellschaft fur Mathematik and Datenverarbeitung (in West Germany), and l'Institut de Recherche d'Informatique et d'Automatique (in France).

The objectives of the joint research are to examine the need for harmonization of legislation, to improve the control of computer data security, and to provide insight into the impact of privacy and security measures. An interim report written in early 1979 commented that most transborder data flow is via physical movement, that is, on cards, tapes and disks.[16]

In early 1980 the European Community announced that it would subsidize the creation of new databases and information-analysis systems for European users as a group. The intent of the subsidization is to contribute to community objectives and to improve information transfer in such matters as public safety and welfare and technological development.

Again, there has been close cooperation by the European Community with the OECD and the Council of Europe. In 1978 the Commission's panel of experts agreed to wait until the Council of Europe had produced its draft convention before proposing legislation binding on the member nations of the European Community. The delay would also provide time to study the effectiveness of the several national laws, which will be covered in the next section of this chapter. The European Parliament, popularly elected for the first time in 1979, was presented in 1980 with a resolution calling for a data control board to be established by the EEC and the national governments of member countries. The board would be modeled after the Swedish Data Inspection Board.

Intergovernmental Bureau for Informatics

The Intergovernmental Bureau for Informatics (IBI), created by UNESCO, began operations in 1961. The IBI is now independent of UNESCO, although it still receives some support from UNESCO and is still, of course, a United Nations agency. The IBI's sole purpose is to be involved in computer/telecommunications issues—informatics—for the public good, that is, to help people understand the impact of informatics on society and to help society realize the maximum benefits of informatics.

In 1978, UNESCO and the IBI jointly sponsored a Conference on Strategies and Policies for Informatics, attended by seventy-eight nations and held in Torremolinos, Spain. The overall conclusions of the conference were that countries should recognize the need for comprehensive informatics policies, that governments should exchange information regarding the stages of informatics experience (especially in regions sharing similar situations), that informatics planning should include the education and training of users and decision makers, that governments should encourage research and a rational use of information systems, and that bilateral arrangements should exist for the sharing of information technology and information resources. The conference also recognized international cooperation as having the utmost importance for the effective utilization of informatics' benefits throughout the world.[17]

The resolutions adopted by the conference also called for standardization of hardware and software, more control over transnational computer and telecommunications companies, and international codes of conduct for marketing and technology transfer. An initiative prepared by the USSR asked for a world software bank to provide standard software. Sixteen African nations jointly sought a program to strengthen the negotiating positions of developing countries in dealing with multinational corporations. France proposed national or regional centers to provide hardware and software maintenance within the geographic regions served by these centers. Benin and Tunisia's resolution sought aid in accessing information about one's own country held abroad (which would give nations the same privacy and access rights as individuals). And Bolivia, Morocco, and Tunisia presented a similar resolution for aid in accessing scientific and technical information stored in databases located beyond national borders.[18]

Transborder data flow was accepted as probably the most important aspect of informatics at the international level. In view of the fact that computer databases in one country might contain comprehensive information about other countries, the conference recommended that UNESCO and the IBI find ways of assuring that transnational transfer of information take place. Another world conference on transborder data flow was scheduled for mid-1980.

The 1978 conference has been characterized as the first of its kind—a worldwide gathering to discuss the social, cultural, political, and technical issues of multinational computer/telecommunications. Reportedly, the debates were less political than many meetings of UN organizations, and the delegates were able to find wide areas for common concern and common action.[19]

Other Agencies

Probably at least a dozen other international agencies or commissions have looked at transborder data flow in some form during the past decade. One such group, the International Institute for Applied Systems Analysis (IIASA), Schloss Laxenburg, Austria, began studying international data exchange and computer networks in 1977. The Institute consulted with representatives of UNESCO, Canada, the United States, and nine Western European countries and concluded that the major long-term considerations are user needs and economic problems such as the impact on jobs, the impact on international balance of payments, and, in general, information infrastructures.[20] The most urgent area for research was deemed to be identification of the major barriers to data exchange. High priority was also given to relating national problems to successful international exchange; finding methods for developing countries to take advantage of data exchange; studying the successes and failures of organizations already engaged in international data exchange; examining the relationship with technology transfer; identifying data network users and their requirements; and discovering organizational structures most appropriate for international data exchange.

Other international organizations also have been concerned with informatics and transborder data flow, although perhaps not to the same extent as the organizations already mentioned. The topic of international computer/tele-communications has, for example, come up in various UN agencies' meetings, including meetings of the International Telecommunications Union, the oldest functioning international organization, founded in 1856. The secretary general of the UN issued a report in 1974 calling on governments to adopt legislation to protect people from the threat posed by computerized information systems. And the secretary general's office and the General Assembly have continued to support investigations of the effects of transborder data traffic and to debate the impact.

National Legislation

Before the international bodies began debating the question of transborder data flow, the issue of personal freedom in an era of computerized information files was already a popular topic. During the 1970s, national laws were enacted in a number of countries to protect personal information stored in or taken from computer files. In some cases, the laws affect the international data traffic as well as the domestic processing and storage. Computer-oriented privacy laws have been passed in Sweden, the United States, West Germany, France, Canada, Finland, Norway, Austria, and Luxembourg and are under discussion elsewhere. But the relationship between transborder data flow and computer data laws, and the impetus behind the legislation in these areas, has not been the same in the countries mentioned.

Sweden

The Swedish situation prior to their data law was one of large centralized data-bases of fairly complete information about almost all citizens. In the early 1970s, information on citizens was held in some five hundred government and forty-five hundred commercial databases. And tapes of these databases were aquirable through "right to know" laws based on long-standing traditions. Corporations, for example, could request from the provincial database the names, addresses, and job descriptions of all residents; a great deal of controversy arose when a large company attempted to do just that. Controversy also arose when the Greek embassy was able to acquire a list of all Greeks living in Sweden. These and dozens of similar incidents led to government inquiries and pressure from the computer industry for legislation (to stave off a backlash effect).[21]

After a series of studies by special commissions, the Swedish Data Act was proposed in 1972, accepted by Parliament in 1973, and became effective in 1974. The law attempts to answer some of the problems by the establishment of a nine-member Data Inspection Board to authorize all databases that identify people (except for government databases, which may only require consultation with the Board) and by ruling that certain kinds of information such as criminal records and psychiatric histories require special permission to store. The law also states that data cannot be transmitted abroad without special permission. In addition, people have the right to see the information about themselves that is on file and to petition for correction if necessary. The law permits the filing of lawsuits by individuals to argue the validity of information.

The Swedish government has continued to investigate the effects of the Data Act and the general information policy. A new Data Act Committee was established in 1976 to review the law, a joint Nordic group was assembled to study the data flow among the Nordic countries (leading to national laws in Denmark and Norway in 1978), a Computer Industry Commission looked at the computer industry itself, the Swedish Telecommunications Administration was urged to develop a public data network, office automation was investigated, and a government commission evaluated viewdata systems (systems in which information in computerized databases can be selected by, and viewed on, home television sets). Because of the studies, according to the director general of the Data Inspection Board, Sweden is still carefully developing any clearcut policy, due to the sweeping effects of computing and information processing.[22]

United States

There is a considerable amount of literature on privacy questions in the United States that was published during the 1960s and 1970s. Rosenberg, in *The Death of Privacy*, details some of the vast collections of data held in U.S. government files and discusses a proposed national-computer system which would have integrated all the government's records on individuals.[23] A report backed by the National Academy of Sciences, published in 1972, concluded that organizations, as a result of computerizing their files, were not collecting more personal information than before and individuals were not suffering from a loss of due process of law.[24] Computerization did, the report found, increase efficiency. Policies protecting personal rights, however, were largely written in precomputer days, and therefore updated policies were nevertheless said to be necessary in the areas of personal privacy, rights of access, limitations on data sharing, and confidentiality of records. Also in 1972, an Advisory Committee on Automated Personal Data Systems, under the direction of the secretary of Health, Education and Welfare, began an analysis of the harmful consequences that might follow the use of computerized databases and of safeguards that might be needed. The report, published the next year, recommended a "Code of Fair Information Practices" based on principles of rights of access, freedom from misuse of data, and knowledge of the extent of computerized files held by all organizations.[25] A *National Information Policy* was published by the Domestic Council Committee on the Rights of Privacy in 1976 outlining policy issues in personal privacy, freedom of information, telecommunications, data processing, and in the use of scientific and technical information.[26] The committee noted that international computer/telecommunications or information technology was blurring the effectiveness of regulatory bodies operating within national boundaries. On the question of transborder data flow, four main themes were outlined: effects on national sovereignty; effects on cultural identification; economic consequences; and citizens' inability to protect their rights regarding databases held in foreign countries.

Although the matter of transborder data traffic has not been specifically addressed in legislation in the United States, related laws have been passed, including the Fair Credit Reporting Act of 1970, the Freedom of Information Act of 1974, the Privacy Act of 1974, and the Right to Financial Privacy Act of 1978. In addition, during the latter part of the decade there occurred a second surge of interest in the computer's effect on the privacy of personal records. A 1978 poll of the U.S. public reported that two out of every three people worry about threats to their privacy and that the federal government was lagging behind in recognizing the public mood.[27] By the end of the next year, 1979, at least six bills had been introduced into Congress regarding data protection, including bills to provide for the protection and confidentiality of medical and research records, to protect personal information in electronic funds transfer (EFT), to limit government access to personal financial records, and to protect personal rights regarding information held by consumer-reporting agencies, credit grantors, credit- and check-authorization agencies, and insurance companies.

West Germany

In West Germany, as in Sweden, the people taking part in the national investigations of the impact of computerized information systems were also generally working with the international organizations such as the Council of Europe and the OECD. The term *data protection* used in many of the international debates is attributed to German origin (datenschutz). State laws for data protection were enacted as early as 1970, when Hesse set regulations governing the use of data, with a Data Protection Commissioner to oversee compliance with the law. This is sometimes considered the very first of all the computer-oriented privacy laws.

The German Federal Data Protection Act was passed in 1976 and took full effect in 1978. The intent of the law is primarily to protect individual freedom by guaranteeing privacy of personal data in information files. The law applies to both electronic and manual filing systems in both the federal and the private sector. However the law does not apply to manual files that are not transmitted to a third party, nor to any information files used for journalistic purposes by press, radio, and television companies. Under the law, a federal commissioner is appointed by the president to monitor federal-agency compliance. Private organizations that employ at least five people in automatic data processing of personal data (or that employ at least twenty people for manual processing of personal data) must appoint a data-protection representative to be responsible for compliance; states are authorized to establish supervisory boards to coordinate the efforts.

In general, in the private sector, organizations may store personal information and may transmit the information if it is in the legitimate interests of the organization and if there is no reason to suppose that the individuals concerned would be harmed by such activity. Personal data that can be proven incorrect must be corrected; if it is impossible to determine either the correctness or the incorrectness of the data, the use or transmission of the data may be blocked and in some cases the data must be erased. People have the right to know what information about them is on file, and where (except in cases of national security, defense, or criminal prosecution). Organizations must ensure that all affected people are aware that information about them is on file. Usually, on paying a fee, a person may have access to data about himself or herself, but exceptions include situations where such access might substantially jeopardize the business aims of the firm or where a third party might be harmed as a result of the access. It is possible that over the next several years, the general nature of the law will be clarified by specific laws for such areas as credit information.[28]

France

The French recognition of the information base of society, referred to generally as *politique de l'informatique,* has been the underlying current running through efforts in computer manufacturing, electronic components manufacturing, telecommunications, and scientific and technical research as a whole. Among the research reports emanating from France was the 1978 *Report on the Computerization of Society* by Simon Nora and Alain Minc.[29] The report primarily addresses a crisis in French society, with the computerization of society being a key issue in that crisis. The authors recommend that European nations form some sort of telecommunications cartel, or joint effort, to establish a dialogue with large computer and telecommunications companies, and with IBM specifically. France is urged to prepare deliberate policy for social change to utilize the benefits of telematics (that is, telecommunications and computers) to influence the international economy and balance of power.

One of the specific results of the Nora Report, as it is called, has been government commitment to the development of banking and finance databases. One French company, DAFSA, owned by most of the large French banks and a marketer of financial and economic information, has been attempting to build such databases domestically, so that U.S. banks would not have a monopoly on the organization of such files.[30]

The French data protection law, the Information Processing, Files and Liberties Act, was promulgated in 1978 to cover databases of information relating to individuals, setting up a National Information and Liberties Commission to administer the law. Authorization is required for public databases that affect private individuals, and a declaration of intent is required for similar private databases. The information in a file must be relevant and must not be kept on file for longer than necessary. Citizens have the right to consent to, or to oppose, the gathering of personal information (subject to other laws governing, for example, criminal matters), and rights of access and rectification are acknowledged. The commission also has the power to impose special safety measures, if warranted, to protect personal information and to regulate the international flow of personal data should dangers arise. The law also prohibits the evaluation of human conduct based solely on automated processing of an individual's profile. This has been remarked as a first attempt in internationally oriented law to legislate social profiles quite beyond personal privacy matters.[31]

Canada

In Canada, a joint task force of the departments of Communications and Justice published *Privacy and Computers* in 1972, concluding that privacy was not the principal problem with computerized information files. The chief problems were, instead, loss of data processing activity within the country and increased national vulnerability as more and more data are stored outside the country, entirely subject to foreign political climates, laws, and judicial proceedings.[32] A year later, another government report noted the problems of jurisdiction with data stored and processed outside the country, especially when the data related to general economic policy

The two concerns, privacy and economic loss, have continued to exist in Canada, although internationally Canada seems to put much more emphasis on the economic questions.[33] On the other hand, a privacy act was in fact enacted in 1977 restricting the use of certain types of information by federal government agencies. The Act does not affect transborder data traffic. Thus the Canadian law is similar to U.S. law and unlike the European data protection laws.

A 1978 position paper in Canada outlined five dangers in international computer/telecommunications, most of which can be called economic dangers, although aspects of privacy and rights of access are also present: loss of employment; balance-of-payments problems; loss of legitimate access to vital records; growing dependence; and decision making by foreign-interest groups.[34] Concerning the loss of jobs, the paper noted that low-paying jobs, for example, data entry, would remain in Canada while the higher level design and decision-making jobs would be drawn off into the information processing centers (presumably in the United States). A Consultative Committee on the Implications for Canadian Sovereignty was formed in 1978 to suggest a restructuring of the entire computer/telecommunications industries. Canadian authorities have estimated that 23,500 data processing jobs might be lost to the United States by 1985, and that $1.5 billion worth of computing services would be imported by then, while the volume of U.S. television and information services flowing into Canada would be increasing.[35] In 1979, a government-appointed committee reiterated the worry in Canada that their proximity to the United States renders their informatics situation especially vulnerable.[36] Canada has continued to emphasize that these concerns for economic and national security, as well as for personal privacy, are legitimate apprehensions about the loss of freedom.

Other Countries

In a number of other countries, primarily in the West or among newly industrialized nations, there have been somewhat similar experiences in trying to forestall any ill effects of computerization and the merging of computer/telecommunications.

Laws in Austria, Denmark, Luxembourg, and Norway have been created governing data protection and personal privacy, but these laws had not come into full effect in early 1980. According to one observer, some of these laws may be restrictive in their applications because the laws cover legal persons, such as business organizations, as well as physical persons, giving the legal persons rights of access to stored data.[37] A proposed Austrian ordinance, for example, would require companies to register all information held regarding competitors, suppliers, and other businesses.

In the United Kingdom, the matter has been under investigation for a decade, but specific legislation has been slow to evolve. A Right of Privacy Bill was introduced in 1970, a government Committee on Privacy published a study in 1972, and the Data Protection Committee published proposed safeguards in 1978. It is perhaps noteworthy that in 1971 a spokesman for International Computers Ltd. (ICL) (Britain's major computer manufacturer) described to an international conference the amounts of information flowing through vast national and international networks; the danger, he said, was to privacy, especially in small countries where national databases can more easily be created and where groups of small countries can more quickly develop international databases.[38]

Australia has been active in the data protection area, where the Law Reform Commission was given the task of investigating privacy problems and the trends in computerized files. The Commission favors international agreements on standards for transborder data flows. An Australian estimate, however, is that the bulk of computer data entering or leaving the country is not moving electronically but physically on magnetic tape and punched cards. The volume of data moving electronically in and out of Australia via telecommunications was judged to be insignificant.[39]

In Brazil, the government established the Planning Council of the Commission for Coordination of Data Processing Activities (CAPRE) in 1976 to monitor the operation of international telecommunications links for data traffic. By virtue of a 1978 resolution, CAPRE requires that all companies seeking to engage in transborder data traffic must secure written permission, renewable every three years. According to the director general of CAPRE, the requirements are in the nature of antitrust legislation to prevent any crippling effects of monopolies and not a form of protectionism that would admittedly encourage inefficiencies and retard development.[40] The underlying principle is that countries like Brazil have a right to become less dependent on other countries, even if it means temporary antimonopoly legislation.

In Portugal, as in Spain, informatics rights are, or will be, part of their respective constitutions. The constitution of Portugal approved in 1977 contains a clause guaranteeing citizens the right to know the contents of databases that relate to themselves. The draft Spanish constitution contains articles limiting the use of data processing to safeguard personal rights.

In sum, the various laws and recommendations described should give an idea of the similarities of concern over individual rights with respect to computerized databases and of the differences (as well as the similarities) with respect to international traffic, concentration of resources and monopolistic practices, and dependence versus independence. Table 2-2 provides a list of countries that have data protection legislation either in effect or under discussion in parliament. Not all the data protection laws affect international information flows.

Issues and Impacts

A great many topics, then, have been advanced in the debates over transborder data flow and the impact of information processing networks and databases.

Table 2-2
Countries with Data Protection Laws

Country	Year of Enactment	Scope
Australia	In process	
Austria	1978, effective 1980	International
Canada	1977	National
Denmark	1978	International
France	1978	International
Luxembourg	1978	International
Netherlands	In process	
New Zealand	1976, 1977	National
Norway	1978	International
Sweden	1973, 1977	International
Switzerland	In process	
United States	1970, 1974, 1976, 1978	National
West Germany	1977	International

Source: Compiled from *Transnational Data Report* 2 (1979): 7, and *Transborder Data Flows*, ed. Rein Turn (Arlington, Virg.: American Federation of Information Processing Societies, 1979), pp. 64-67.

A survey of articles in a handful of computer magazines for 1977 and 1978 indicates that all the topics could be grouped under three major headings: economic problems, dependence problems, and privacy problems.[41] But these are not clean divisions. Dependency problems are also economic, privacy problems can be economic as well when the information is proprietary business data or the plaintiff is a legal entity, economic problems themselves can fall in either of the other two categories, and there is no mention of cultural concerns that go beyond the balance-of-payments question.

Despite the inability to clearly and authoritatively set out the major categories or issues, the review of the literature for the present study indicates that there are indeed a few subsurface (and sometimes explicit) themes running throughout the debates in the various countries among the numerous participants. The two most prominent themes seem to be: (1) a belief that information is definitely a key resource and information processing a key activity in present and near-future society; and (2) a strong desire for some legal mechanism that would be truly international. As table 2-3 indicates, some of the topics discussed fall more under one theme than the other, and other topics appear to share both themes.

The second theme follows from the first, given the existence of the multinational computer networks. And it is the second theme that may be the most powerful and far reaching. Most of the issues listed in table 2-3 can be expressed in terms of a desire for legal protection—protection of privacy, protection of access rights, protection of economic sectors, protection from misuse of data

Table 2-3
Issues Underlying Transborder Data Flow Themes

Information as Key Resource or Key Activity	Need for International Legal Mechanism
Resource monitoring	Protecting personal privacy
Health information	Nontariff trade barriers
Science research	Data havens, pirate databases
Technology transfer	Control by multinationals
Timesharing services	Common carrier interconnections
International communication	Customs laws and taxes
Computer technician training	Police agency cooperation
	Press freedom
	Broadcasting

Protecting nonpersonal data
Threats to national sovereignty
Dependence
Labor shifts
Economic planning, growth
Worldwide telecommunications planning
Database use
Balance of payments

laws, protection from lack of cooperative legal machinery. Many of the articles and speeches in the transborder data flow debates have either urged laws to prevent abuses or argued against proposed laws because they might be misapplied, but the message is the same: in the international arena, there are few ready and efficient means for balancing conflicts between citizens and organizations who, while in different countries, are interacting with each other almost instantaneously via computer/telecommunications.

Eventually, this second theme may be recognized as the most important social impact of the use of computerized information systems across national borders. This is, the rise of transnational networks for computing and information processing in the 1960s and 1970s did not cause interdependence but did encourage and perhaps foster the desire among political leaders, business leaders, and scholars for cooperative nonmilitary means for relegating national boundaries to a minor position in the international problem-solving process. At present, it is still too early to tell with any degree of certainty.

Within this framework, then, of transborder data flows and international attempts at cooperation and harmonization, a more specific area, namely the use of international networks by multinational corporations, can be singled out for more intense study, since the multinational corporations are apparently the largest nonmilitary users of such networks.[42] In the following chapter, attention will be concentrated on one particular industry, international banking, within the context of international interdependence.

Notes

1. "U.S. Computer Control from Britain," *Times* (London), 4 January 1963, p. 6.

2. H.F. Mitchell, Jr., "The Future of the Switching Computer," *Datamation* April 1965, pp. 24-25.

3. Walter E. Simonson, "Data Communications: The Boiling Pot," *Datamation*, April 1967, pp. 22-25.

4. Robert B. Forest, "Close Cooperation: Europe's Best Hope," *Datamation*, 15 December 1971, pp. 22-28.

5. Ithiel de Sola Pool, "Background Report," in *Conference on Computer/Telecommunications Policy* (Paris: Organization for Economic Cooperation and Development, 1975), pp. 281-308.

6. Edwin Parker, "Background Report," in *Conference on Computer/Telecommunications Policy* (Paris: Organization for Economic Cooperation and Development, 1975), pp. 88-104.

7. "Conclusions," in *Conference on Computer/Telecommunications Policy* (Paris: Organization for Economic Cooperation and Development, 1975), pp. 13-16.

8. H.P. Gassmann, "The Activities of the OECD in the Field of Trans-

national Data Regulation," in *Data Regulation. European and Third World Realities* (Uxbridge (U.K.): Online Conferences, 1978), pp. 180-181.

9. Russell G. Pipe, "International Treaty on Data Protection, Privacy in Limbo," *Computerworld*, 28 January 1980, pp. 20-21, 25.

10. Jake Kirchner, "OECD Meets in Paris to Head Off Piecemeal Data Flow Legislation," *Computerworld*, 15 October 1979, p. 3.

11. *The Usage of International Data Networks in Europe* (Paris: Organization for Economic Cooperation and Development, 1979).

12. F.W. Hondius, "The Work of the Council of Europe in the Area of Data Protection," in *Data Regulation* (Uxbridge (U.K.): Online Conferences, 1978), p. 62.

13. Frits Hondius, "Council of Europe Nearing Completion of Treaty on International Data Protection and Privacy," *Computerworld*, 21 January 1980, pp. 18-19.

14. Frank Carmody, "The Work of the European Community in the Area of Computers and Privacy," in *Data Regulation* (Uxbridge (U.K.): Online Conferences, 1978), pp. 105-112.

15. Nancy Foy, "Computer Policy for the Common Market," *Datamation*, June 1973, p. 139.

16. GMD-IRIA-NCC, "Joint Report on Data Security and Confidentiality, Interim Report," April 1979, p. 4.

17. F.A. Bernasconi, "Informatics Integral to a New International Economic and Information Order," in *Data Regulation* (Uxbridge (U.K.): Online Conferences, 1978), pp. 115-117.

18. E. Drake Lundell, Jr., "SPIN Nations Hammer Out Details of New World Order," *Computerworld* 11 September 1978, pp. 1,4.

19. E. Drake Lundell, Jr., "Criticisms of IBM Muted but Evident at Meeting," *Computerworld*, 11 September 1978, p. 6.

20. D. Penniman, A. Butrimenko, and J. Page, "International Data Exchange and the Application of Informatics Technology" (Paper prepared for the International Institute for Applied Systems Analysis, Austria, December 1977).

21. "Sweden Regulates Those Snooping Data Banks," *Business Week*, 6 October 1973, pp. 93-95.

22. Jan Freese, "The Present and Future Swedish Data Policy," in *Data Regulation* (Uxbridge (U.K.): Online Conferences, 1978), pp. 83-84.

23. Jerry M. Rosenberg, *The Death of Privacy* (New York: Random House, 1969).

24. Alan F. Westin and Michael A. Baker, *Databanks in a Free Society* (New York: Quadrangle, New York Times Book Co., 1972).

25. U.S. Department of Health, Education and Welfare, Advisory Committee on Automated Personal Data Systems, *Records, Computers and the Rights of Citizens* (Boston: Massachusetts Institute of Technology, 1973).

26. Domestic Council Committee on the Rights of Privacy, *National*

Information Policy (Washington, D.C.: National Commission on Libraries and Information Science, 1976).

27. David Burnham, "Poll Finds Increasing Concern over Threats to Privacy," *New York Times,* 4 May 1979, p. A19.

28. Rudolf Schomerus, "The German Federal Data Protection Act," in *Data Regulation* (Uxbridge (U.K.): Online Conferences, 1978), pp. 85-92.

29. Simon Nora and Alain Minc, *Report on the Computerization of Society,* (Paris: Board of Financial Examiners, 1978), introduction; see also "The Nora Report—Report on the Computerization of Society," *TDF News,* November 1978, p. 7.

30. Edith Holmes, "French Commit Funds to Develop Database Industry," *Information World,* August 1979, p. 1.

31. "Focus on France," *Transnational Data Report,* March 1978, p. 3.

32. See Oswald H. Ganley, "The Role of Communications and Information Resources in Canada," Harvard University Program on Information Resources Policy, June 1979, p. 10.

33. William Serwatynski, "Transborder Dataflow—Lifeblood of Multinationals," *Information Privacy* 1 (November 1978): 82.

34. See Oswald H. Ganley, "The Role of Communications and Information Resources in Canada," Harvard University Program on Information Resources Policy, June 1979.

35. Angeline Pantages, "Canada's Economic Concerns," *Datamation,* 1 November 1978, pp. 67-75.

36. *TDF News,* May 1979, p. 1.

37. G. Russell Pipe, "International Treaty on Data Protection, Privacy in Limbo," *Computerworld,* 28 January 1980, pp. 20-21, 25.

38. Arthur L.C. Humphreys, "The British/Western European Viewpoint," in *Expanding the Use of Computers in the 70s,* ed. Fred Gruenberger (Englewood Cliffs, N.J.: Prentice-Hall, 1971), pp. 69-82.

39. G. Russell Pipe, "Australians Favor International Privacy Accord," *Computerworld,* 7 November 1977, p. 17.

40. Ricardo A.C. Saur, "Information, New Technologies and Data Regulation," in *Data Regulation* (Uxbridge (U.K.): Online Conferences, 1978), pp. 223-233.

41. William Serwatynski, "Transborder Dataflow: A Global View," *Information Privacy* 1 (January 1979): 133-136; and "Transborder Dataflow—Lifeblood of Multinationals," *Information Privacy* 1 (November 1978): 81-86.

42. See *Data Networks in Europe* (Paris: Organization for Economic Cooperation and Development, 1979); and Richard H. Veith, "Informatics and Transborder Data Flow: The Question of Social Impact," *Journal of the American Society for Information Science* 31 (March 1980): 105-110.

3 Computers, Networks, and Banks

When the first experimental telephone exchange began operation, in Boston in 1877, there were three corporate clients—one a banking firm.[1] Since that time the banking industry has continued to incorporate improvements in telecommunications, and in computers, to such an extent that in some cases banking is now preeminently an electronic function. Internationally, computer networks have been established within individual banking organizations and also as joint undertakings among groups of banking organizations. In addition, many banks use the services of timesharing bureaus for access to databases, for data communications, and for data storage.

Banking has been chosen as the subject of this research because the set of multinational electronic information networks in international banking seems to involve directly the greatest number of participating organizations exchanging a high volume of information. According to the data-traffic survey conducted for the Organization for Economic Cooperation and Development (OECD), the international airline network probably carries the greatest volume of any single network, but it involves only twenty organizations' reservation systems (although each of these twenty may serve other airlines as clients).[2] The airlines network in 1979 connected an estimated eighteen hundred agent terminals around the world. The banking network, on the other hand, connected nearly seven hundred member organizations and thousands of terminals, even though the estimated volume was one-fourth to one-third that of the airline network.[3] There is also a difference between the two networks in the impact of the traffic. The airline network is largely used for seat reservations; agents are interacting with a list of available seats rather than directly with other people in other organizations. But the banking network is used for messages sent directly to other organizations causing the receiver to take action on behalf of clients, that is, the impact seems more immediate and of greater consequence.

In another sense, banking offers a unique opportunity because of the very nature of some of the messages, namely money. The international flowing of funds information electronically has, according to some, resulted in the phenomena of money without a country and a supranational banking system.[4] Although this book is not intended to be an economic analysis of currency and credit systems, the uniqueness of the banking situation will be taken into account in relating the use of multinational networks to the functioning of the user organizations.

To explain more fully the extent of transborder information systems in banking, it is necessary to review briefly automation in banking generally (in the United States, although the story is similar in other industrialized countries). This review will also touch on the growth of multinational corporations as well as multinational banks and will describe the variety of computer/telecommunications networks in banking.

Automation

Mechanization in banking, of course, preceded computerization. Punched cards and primitive sorters were available for banking use in the 1930s. In fact, check handling and deposit accounting were partially mechanized in almost all U.S. banks by 1940. It was only a matter of time, then, before the computer would be brought in to upgrade the earlier equipment and to solve problems caused by the growing volume of paperwork.

The first computer for commercial use was built in the United States from 1946 to 1950, and soon several of the largest banks were investigating ways to utilize the computer in attacking paperwork problems. San Francisco-based Bank of America began working with the Stanford Research Institute around 1950 to find ways of automating check processing, using some form of bar coding. A trade journal reported in 1965 that it had been the Bank of America, with one large order, that had put General Electric in the computer business.[5] In the early 1950s, New York's Citibank's precursor was also investigating automation, in a joint project with ITT.

There were a number of reasons why banks were strongly interested in automation, but the chief reason was the immense proliferation of checks from 1939 to 1952 and particularly after World War II. The massive increase has been attributed to a basic change in banking philosophy to a more "retail" approach, to changes in spending habits, and to the beginning of a genuine national economy.[6] Along with the volume of paper processing, banks were faced with labor shortages in what were low-paying jobs with very high turnover.

Beginning in 1945, the American Banking Association (ABA) and the Federal Reserve System began the use of standard routing symbols on checks; in 1954, the ABA decided to try to standardize the mechanical aspects of check handling, forming the Mechanization of Check Handling subcommittee of the ABA's Bank Management Commission. Surveys were conducted, technical reports prepared, and various proposed systems evaluated. Finally in 1958 the committee published its report leading to the uniform use of magnetic ink characters (MICR encoding) on the face of checks to contain standard routing information, the amount of the check, the account number, and inhouse codes. Meanwhile, the first electronic computer had been installed in a commercial bank in 1955, and the automation of banking had begun.

Actually, the computerization of banking on any sort of scale is said to have begun around 1960 and there was a dramatic proliferation of computers in banks from 1960 to 1964.[7] It is interesting, though, to find that in the mid-1960s, bankers and computer people were not considered to be especially friendly to each other—computer personnel thought bankers naive and confused, and bankers apparently felt that the computer industry did not really understand what was happening.[8]

Automation Studies

A number of studies of computers and automation in U.S. banks have been published, the ABA periodically conducts automation surveys and convenes conferences on automation in banking, trade journals often report the "latest" in computer systems in one bank or another, and numerous studies have been undertaken in the area of what is now called electronic funds transfer (EFT).

Aldom et al., in a 1963 book, addressed the effects of automation on the banking industry as a whole and the effects on individual banks, tracing the need for automation, the development of MICR coding, the effects on smaller banks, and legal considerations.[9] The book foresaw a central role for Federal Reserve Banks in the automated movement of money instruments and a broadening of banking services through the use of computers. Aldom expected that in the future there would be organizational changes accompanying the increased use of data processing systems.

A dissertation on banking automation, by Yavitz in 1964, attempted to present a conceptual scheme, or model, for analyzing the impact of automation.[10] Commercial banking was selected as the object of inquiry because, as an industry, it was perceived as being well defined and quite homogeneous. Yavitz conducted interviews and inspections at eight banks, used data compiled by Booz, Allen and Hamilton, Inc. (management consultants), used data collected in the ABA's 1963 automation survey, and interviewed other bankers and researchers. Dramatic impacts of automation were simply not found, and the four case studies presented in the book indicated that the proposed levels of automation did not explain or predict impact.

Regarding automation's impact on separate areas such as employment, organizational structure, managerial responsibilities, and banking services, little evidence of radical impact was found.[11] The most evident impact was in the area of employment, with larger volumes of paperwork handled per employee, but the evidence was still not dramatic. Many banks, for example, made it a matter of policy not to lay off employees as a result of automation. Few changes in organizational structure were attributed to automation, except perhaps for temporary advisory committees during the initial automation process. However, despite the lack of obvious impact on structure overall, Yavitz suggested that when the automation of decision making occurred at a high level, major changes in the decision-making process, and thus in organizational structure, could be anticipated.

James Vaughan and Avner Porat, in research partly sponsored by the Federal Deposit Insurance Corporation (FDIC), continued in the Yavitz tradition and concentrated on small and medium-size banks, looking for changes in banking organizations associated with the introduction of computers.[12] Fifty-seven banks, a modified random sample, were studied through field interviews and questionnaires (710 were mailed, 62 percent were returned and used). Data from FDIC records and several ABA automation surveys were used as well.

Generally, changes in banks' information systems were found to occur much more rapidly than changes in the structure of the organization. Although it might be expected that the supplying of more information faster and in more formats, which was taking place, would permit more analysis and interpretation by managers, this was seen by bankers to be still in the future.[13] Overall, only 35 percent of the respondents thought that their range of decision making had increased after computer systems were installed.

In the larger banks, computers did seem to change the lines of informal authority, but formal acknowledgment of the change was slow to follow. About 30 percent of the respondents thought that the use of the computer was breaking down areas of functional responsibility, but about half the respondents disagreed. The computer was having little perceived effect on officers' communication patterns, although officers at the lower levels seemed to think that that would not be true for long. Chief-executive officers almost unanimously agreed that the computer permitted a better grasp of the entire bank's activities and therefore better management control. The computer was able to provide existing reports more quickly and more accurately and also was able to provide some new types of information.[14] Regarding decision making specifically, managers reported that decisions were being made at the same levels as before. Nevertheless, Vaughan and Porat concluded that that was a short-term result, that in fact the kinds of decisions made at each level were changing. Since all the banks in the 1969 study were still in the early stages of computerization, the authors felt that the most exciting phase, the application of computerized management science techniques, was still to come.

Following the lead of Aldom, Yavitz, Vaughan and Porat, and others, a set of theses on the impact of the computer in banking was published in 1975, based on a 1972 questionnaire.[15] Although there were admittedly problems with the questionnaire itself (it was so long that a large number were not returned or were returned incomplete), the combined theses do provide some additional insights into the use of computers in banking.

Reviewing the history of banks' use of computers, one thesis established, as might be expected, that the computer was introduced into the larger banks first and only later to medium-size banks and then to the smaller banks.[16] Of the larger banks (those with assets over $500 million), some 92 percent had their own computer installations by 1963. Of all banks, though, only about 56 percent were using computers when the ABA conducted an automation survey nine years later.

Another thesis examined the computer's impact on organizational structure more closely, although the data came from only thirty-six banks and twenty-four of those banks had assets of less than $200 million.[17] Two-thirds of the responding banks indicated an increase in the number of organizational levels or in the total number of departments that had accompanied computerization, with the chances for increase being greater among the larger banks with inhouse computer systems. But on the question of organizational level alone, twenty banks stated that there was no change.

A third thesis looked at the impact on internal operations and reported that the computer had its greatest impact on already highly centralized banks.[18] For example, salary increases and promotions could be based on reports from the branches showing performance against budget levels, and preparation of the general ledger could be done at the head office for the entire organization, if the organization was already inclined toward centralized management. The computer was described as being especially useful for information exchange between foreign branches and the home office. Particularly, the computer could be used to keep track of exchange rates, the date of the exchange rate being used, any adjustments required, and any reports that needed to be generated for regulatory agencies. Again, the greatest impact was believed to be still in the future.

Information Technology

The computerization of banks has continued to such an extent that some of the larger banks are recognized leaders in information processing technology, with their own research and development arms and database subsidiaries, even though, according to the 1978 ABA automation survey, 20 percent of U.S. banks are still not using computers.[19] The computerization of banking has led, for example, to the electronic transfer of funds not only among banks, or between banks and corporate clients, but also between banks and the general public.

Corporate clients, for example, can use electronic cash management programs in which the company's computer terminals (or telephone or telex) can be used to get information immediately from the bank regarding ledger balances, funds to be collected, total debits and credits, lockbox deposits, and wire transfers. Such programs, or computer software, can be used throughout the world. Chemical Bank's cash management information systems, for instance, are used by some 300 customers in 24 countries. Included in the systems offered by Chemical Bank is a specific program for foreign exchange transactions that will automatically, on command, buy currency and debit and credit the proper accounts. In addition, the transfers may be routed via one of the automated networks discussed later in this chapter, such as the Fed Wire or CHIPS.

The general public's contacts with electronic banking come in the form of online teller machines, automated teller terminals, point-of-sale terminals, and pay-by-phone services. A 1979 survey indicated that about 15 percent of banks were online, with some 6200 automated teller machines, about 10,500 point-of-sale terminals in use nationwide, and 1,150 banks providing some form of telephone-banking service.[20] These figures are projected to increase to 18,250 automated teller machines and 150,000 point-of-sale terminals by 1981, with 93 percent of all commercial banks using automated teller machines by 1980.[21] A survey by Frost and Sullivan, Inc., market researchers, reportedly states that telephone-bill paying is currently offered by 150 financial institutions nationally, with 1,535 such systems expected by 1989.[22] The most advanced at-home banking systems are not expected to find a ready market until the 1990s. For other countries, the number of automated teller machines in Europe in 1978 was estimated at 5,480; and in Japan that estimated number was 10,750, Japan being near saturation.[23]

Along with traditional banking services, banks offer information services such as online databases of economic indicators or foreign trade statistics, as well as computer processing and related software such as the cash management program mentioned before. A survey of approximately one hundred banks with assets over $100 million determined that 27.3 percent of the banks sell computer time, 20.4 percent sell software packages, and 63.4 percent sell some computer services to correspondent banks.[24] Among the database offerings are those produced by the Bank of America, Citibank, Chase Manhattan Bank, and the Federal Reserve Bank of San Francisco. The database offerings of Chase Manhattan Bank, for example, marketed through a subsidiary (Interactive Data Corporation), include programs to divide, combine, or otherwise process the database to produce customized files or answers based on complex calculations. A trade newsletter suggests that the programs developed by Interactive Data Corporation could be considered models for the entire database industry.[25]

In the internal operations of banks, computers and information systems are part of the "information age" trend in office automation—the paperless office with enhanced tools for decision making. Citibank, for example, set out to fully automate all its offices with electronic word processing, electronic mail, local-office computing power, multimedia archival files, message switching and distribution, electronic conferencing, and broadband point-to-point communications. During the preliminary studies, it was confirmed that managers spend most of their time communicating, but it was also discovered that administrators engage in a lot of information checking or verifying activity, that is, communicating with a database, not with a person.[26]

The central concept in Citibank's automated office is the minicomputer/ desktop-terminal combination called a *workstation*. More importantly, the workstation is to be supported by vertically integrated information systems, so that one workstation's operators can provide all banking services to a particular set of customers. In about ten years, Citibank considers that it will be feasible to have at least one workstation in every Citibank office, or perhaps twenty to forty thousand workstations in four thousand offices.[27] Reportedly, Citibank began the push to automate offices at the beginning of the 1970s in response to costs growing faster than earnings. Even though the prototype workstations were not as welcome to managers as the bank had hoped, the introduction of the workstation concept continues with a combination of decentralization and customer orientation. Along with the technical changes, the bank has made organizational changes. Beginning in 1980, Citibank is to have only two major groups within the organization: banking services for corporations, governments, and institutions; and banking services for individuals. Each group will be worldwide but will be highly decentralized internally.

Citibank is also now a manufacturer of the advanced automated office systems through purchase of Lexar Corporation in 1979. In addition, the bank conducts research and development in electronic banking devices through ownership of Transaction Technology, Inc. Citibank has also proposed the establishment of a new subsidiary, Citishare, which would provide information processing services internationally for financial modeling, loan and investment analysis, and similar activities.

Citibank may be one of the more publicized users of the computer (and minicomputers and microprocessors) in banking, but they are not alone. Most of the larger banks have been proceeding along similar lines. Chase Manhattan's Advanced Systems Technology Division, Manufacturers Hanover Trust, Bankers Trust, Bank of America, Wells Fargo Bank, and Continental Illinois Bank and Trust Company are just a few of the banks which have been mentioned in trade journals, magazines, and newspapers for their advances in information systems. At Continental Illinois, as a trade newspaper relates, there have been not only efforts at more computerization but also efforts to allow employees to work from home.[28] Fifteen or twenty of the bank's senior managers have terminals in their homes and word-processing stations have been placed in a number of lower-level employees' homes for the more routine typing and editing chores.

Interdependence

To look at automated banking across national borders, it is necessary to consider, at least, the post-World War II growth of multinational corporations and multinational banking and the rise of computer/telecommunications networks in banking.

Since 1945, the growth of multinational corporations has been remarkable,

leading to increased economic interdependence, especially among the developed
market economies. Between 1950 and 1967, U.S. manufacturing and petroleum
investment in Europe, for example, increased over ten times its original size.[29]
And along with U.S. multinationals, European and Japanese corporations have
also expanded. The process has been called a two-way street, in which internationally expanding firms also lose part of their domestic market to foreign competition. More recently, multinational corporations from developing countries
are also gaining prominence. In a recent partial listing of the five hundred
largest non-U.S. multinationals, there were thirty-four companies from developing countries.[30] And some of the largest third world multinationals were not
on the list. Perhaps more importantly, there has been a strong surge of supra-
nationalism among the developing countries, a collective spirit of self-reliance.[31]

International banking has more or less followed the expansion of multinational corporations, although banking was international almost from the
very beginning of the institution, circa 1000 A.D. Bankers quickly settled
outside their home countries to serve clients better, to simplify funds transfers, to meet the requirements of international trade that began expanding in
the thirteenth century, and to profit from differences in exchange rates.[32]

For U.S. banks, there was little expansion outside of the country prior
to World War II. There were only six or seven banks with about one hundred
foreign branches or offices prior to 1940. As table 3-1 indicates, Chase National
Bank opened its first overseas branch in London in 1887 with a handful of
other banks slowly following. However, it was the development of telecommunications services that permitted foreign branches to function effectively on a
grand scale.[33]

Table 3-1
Early Overseas Offices of U.S. Banks

Bank	Overseas Location	Year
Chase National Bank	London	1887
	Paris	1910
Guaranty Trust	London	1897
	Paris	1917
National City Bank	London	1902
American Express Banking Corporation	London	1920
Bankers Trust	London	1922
First National Bank of Boston	London	1922
Central Hanover Bank	London	1925
Bank of America	London	1932

Source: Compiled from Stuart Robinson, Jr., *Multinational Banking*
(Leiden: A.W. Sijthoff, 1972), p. 15; and "Foreign Banks in London,"
The Banker (November 1978): 65-129.

Stuart Robinson, in a 1969 book, delineates three waves of expansion of U.S. banks abroad: 1945 to 1958; 1959 to 1963 (the first Eurodollar operating phase following the 1959 European Monetary Agreement); and 1963 to 1967 (the second Eurodollar phase following attempts by President Kennedy to dampen capital outflow). Table 3-2, compiled from the annual reports of the Federal Reserve Board and the annual reports of the Comptroller of the Currency, shows a steady growth in the number of foreign branches or offices beginning in 1945 (after a decline during the war), which rises rather sharply

Table 3-2
Growth of Foreign Operations of U.S. Banks

Year	Number of Banks[a]	Number of Offices or Branches[b]	Number of Branches by Region					Total Number of Countries or Territories
			Europe	Latin America	Near East	Far East	Africa	
1938	7	101						23
1939	7	92						22
1940	7	93						23
1945	7	72						20
1950	7	95	15	49		19		24
1955	7	111	17	56	4	20		26
1961	8	135(135)	18	62	3	25	3	35
1962		(145)						
1963	10	160(160)	26	73	4	31	3	42
1964		(180)						
1965	13	211(210)	42	88	5	50	2	50
1966	13	244(244)	47	102	6	57	2	53
1967	15	295(291)	58	133	6	63	3	54
1968	26	373(374)	80	177	6	72	3	57
1969	53	460(460)	103	235	6	77	1	59
1970	79	532(536)						66
1971	91	577(577)						67
1972	107	627(627)						73
1973	125	699(694)						76
1974	125	732(726)						79
1975	126	762(762)						83
1976	126	731(728)[c]						85
1977	130	738						84
1978	137	761						

Source: Data compiled from the U.S. Board of Governors of the Federal Reserve System Annual Reports, and the U.S. Comptroller of the Currency Annual Reports, for the years listed.

[a]Member banks of the Federal Reserve System only.

[b]Number in parentheses indicate all foreign branches, derived from the Comptroller of the Currency's *Annual Report 1976*.

[c]The loss in the number of branches resulted from 30 branches in Colombia becoming subsidiaries to conform to Colombian law.

in the early 1960s and slows down in the latter part of the 1970s. The number
of different countries or territories nearly doubled from 1950 to 1963 and
doubled again by 1976. The breakdown by regions of the world, for the years
available, shows that the largest number of branches or foreign offices of U.S.
banks has been, and continues to be, in Latin America, although the proportion of European operations has been steadily growing, particularly since the
mid-1960s.

A variety of factors have affected why and in what manner banks choose
to expand internationally. A 1959 Bank of America document explains that
in Europe, representatives established direct corporate relations with European
multinationals to maintain and expand European operations, in the Philippines
the bank was invited in, in Japan the bank was one of three U.S. and three
British banks brought in by military authorities after the war, and in Bangkok
and Hong Kong the expansion resulted from a market study of banking opportunities.[34] Government policy and legislation have also been responsible for
the outward spread of U.S. banks. The Interest Equalization Tax in 1963, the
Voluntary Foreign Credit Restraint program imposed by the Federal Reserve
in 1965, and the mandatory controls program in 1968 all had the effect of
impelling banks to establish branches overseas.[35] The foreign activities of the
larger U.S. banks have become so important to total operations that in 1976
seven of the largest U.S. banks earned over half of their total earnings from
their international operations, although none did in 1970.[36] (See table 3-3.)
Part of the reason for the shift was the beginning of the energy crisis and the
subsequent movement of "oil money."

Soon after U.S. banks began expanding abroad on a large scale, other
countries' banks were entering the U.S. market—part of the broader pattern
of multinational business development.[37] As was the case with the U.S. banks,

Table 3-3
Proportion of Foreign Earnings for Major U.S. Banks

	International Earnings as Percentage of Total Earnings	
Bank Company	1970	1976
Citicorp	40.0	72
Chase Manhattan	22.0	78
Manufacturers Hanover	13.0	56
J.P. Morgan	25.0	53
Bankers Trust	14.5	64
Charter New York (Irving Trust)	12.0	58
First National, Boston	8.0	65

Source: Compiled from *The Economist*, 14 January 1978, p. 99.

there were foreign branches from other nations in the United States in the nineteenth century (the Bank of Montreal opened a U.S. office in 1859, and the British company, the Hong Kong and Shanghai Banking Group, opened in 1879), but the real growth occurred in the 1960s. From approximately 21 foreign banks in New York in 1913 to approximately 30 in 1951 there was only slow growth. However, following a 1961 law favoring foreign branch banking in the United States—enacted partly because of complaints from other countries about lack of reciprocal opportunities—the number of foreign banks jumped to 160 by mid-1975[38] and to 290 by mid-1978.[39] The reasons behind the increase have been extremely varied.[40] Nevertheless, a U.S. Department of Commerce study concluded that although the reasons differ significantly from country to country, factors favoring expansion by foreign banks in the early 1970s were a strong loan demand in the United States, a sharp expansion of money supplies in the industrialized countries, and fears that the United States might place restrictions on expansion.[41]

The effects of foreign expansion, especially by non-U.S. banks into the United States, have been the subject of both government and private inquiries. A study of foreign branches in the United States concludes that one effect has been the stimulation of competition.[42] The result has been more beneficial than harmful; in fact, the study went on, the good effects far outweigh any negative effects. Another study by a private corporation has concluded that U.S. banks are more active overseas than foreign banks are in the United States and that foreign banks in the United States are pursuing only limited goals.[43]

The relationship between telecommunications (and computer services) and all this expansion has been noted on numerous occasions. Robinson suggests that the computer transfer of accounts could well affect the most basic aspects of international banking.[44] When foreign branches came into existence on a wide scale, a telephone call or telex message to a branch bank could often accomplish in a few minutes what might have taken at least a day through a correspondent bank. Foreign exchange dealings have, since the spread of telephone systems, come to rely heavily on telephone commitments, backed up by exchange of a written document later. Martin Mayer, in *The Bankers*, describes money rushing around the world at a furious pace, where entire cycles of borrowing and depositing can take place every fifteen minutes or so.[45]

There is also a flow of information brought about by the use of computer processing, which takes place because of the regulatory systems for banking. The Office of the Comptroller of the Currency in the United States has a special unit for examining foreign data processing centers. Four such centers were examined in 1972, fifteen were examined in 1975, and thirteen in 1976, for example. The international examiners look over the quality of international loans and investment portfolios, accounting and record-keeping systems, and the adequacy of internal control and audit programs. In 1975, when two of the largest U.S. banks decentralized their credit supervision into regional centers, examiners from the comptroller's office joined with bank personnel to develop together the information-collecting systems for the foreign branches. The International Banking Group of the comptroller's office also works with bank supervisors from Canada, Japan, Western Europe, Australia, and the Far East, assisting each other and exchanging ideas.

Other agencies collect information on international banking as well. The Federal Reserve Board began collecting monthly information on foreign branches of U.S. banks in 1969 and extended the coverage in 1975. And in 1978 the U.S. Treasury expanded the scope of its data collection on foreign lending by banks in the United States. Some of the leading sources of data on international bank lending now include the *U.S. Treasury Bulletin*, the *Federal Reserve Bulletin*, and other Federal Reserve Board publications, publications of the Bank for International Settlements, the Bank of England *Quarterly Bulletin*, the Deutsche Bundesbank's *Monthly Reports*, the Bank of Japan's *Economic Statistics Monthly,* and World Bank publications.[46]

Bank Networks

The banking industry utilizes a complete mix of telecommunications facilities and computer networks, using the services of common carriers, specialized carriers, cable television, and so on, who in turn use a full range of hardware from satellites to optical fibers. Networks for banking use include private networks for single organizations, an industry network for international exchanges, various types of national and regional networks, shared use of commercial timesharing networks, and numerous configurations using dial-up access.

Domestic Networks

Within the United States, the Federal Reserve System's network, Fed Wire, serves all Federal Reserve District Banks and their branches, with a central switching computer in Culpepper, Virginia. Although wire transfer facilities had been in use since the 1930s, the process of automating the network did not begin until 1971. The network carried approximately 110,000 messages a day in late 1979 and is said to be growing at a rate of 20 percent annually. Thirty-five of the banks on Fed Wire are connected directly through their computers rather than through remote terminals. Sometime in the early 1980s, Fed Wire will begin converting the network to packet switching technology, a process whereby messages are divided into small "packets" of data, error-checked, supplemented with address and sequence information, and individually routed through different paths to the same destination.

A second network is the nongovernment Bank Wire, cooperatively owned by about two hundred banks. The network is operated by Payment and Telecommunications Services Corporation and carries some 20,000 messages a day. There are several differences between this network and Fed Wire. Fed Wire is essentially free to banks—there is no direct charge except for transactions under $1000—and Bank Wire charges 60 cents per message. Bank Wire, however, offers more services, such as the ability to send administrative messages. Another difference is that Fed Wire can give immediate availability of funds, but Bank Wire carries only messages resulting in debits or credits for existing accounts, but not the actual availability of funds. Bank Wire has recently been interconnected with the telex network to allow telex subscribers to receive messages that way. In addition, in 1979 Bank Wire began working with the Interbank Card Association, one of the major U.S. credit card organizations, to provide the interchange facility among banks in the credit card system.

A third U.S. banking network is the Clearing House Interbank Payments System (CHIPS), linking over 350 computer terminals at ninety-two banks in the New York City area. CHIPS was established in 1970 after a committee of the New York Clearing House banks determined that it was the best way to handle rapidly growing volumes of interbank payments and to meet the need to control increasing credit risks. Message volume on CHIPS is about 46,000 messages on an average day, with an average daily dollar volume of $120 million.

Since many banks place all their money transfer activities on a single in-house computer, the use of the various networks can be automatically coordinated. A foreign transfer coming into the United States may come into a given bank via CHIPS, go out via Bank Wire, and be advised via SWIFT, the international network for exchanging funds information.[47] There are presently indications that the Federal Reserve Board may link Fed Wire to SWIFT, which would provide an alternative to using CHIPS for international payments.

SWIFT

The Society for Worldwide Interbank Financial Telecommunication (SWIFT) was founded in May 1973 by 240 European, U.S., and Canadian banks, after studies that began in 1969. The network is a cooperative society under Belgian law and is wholly owned by member banks. The network did not actually become operational until May 1977, reportedly because of serious delays in software development. There are about 680 member banks in twenty-six countries, exchanging over 170,000 messages a day (not all member banks are yet connected to the network, though). By the end of 1982, a daily volume of

350,000 messages is expected. In addition to the original system of dual operating centers in Amsterdam and Brussels, a third computer center was recently built in the United States near the Fed Wire computer-switching center 65 miles southwest of Washington, D.C.

In 1979, the country with the most banking organizations connected to SWIFT was West Germany, followed by Italy and the United States. (See table 3-4.) The Austrian banks were relatively the most active users, sending 60 percent of their international transactions via SWIFT although the West German banks accounted for the greatest absolute volume (413,000 messages per month) followed by the United States (374,000 messages per month).[48]

Member banks connect their terminals to regional processors in each country, which in turn are tied to the operating centers. The operating centers are complete replications of each other so that one may handle the entire load if another is disabled.

Table 3-4
Number of Banking Organizations Belonging
to SWIFT, by Country

Country	Number of Member Banks
West Germany	108
Italy	100
United States	85
Switzerland	51
France	50
Japan	42
Austria	34
Denmark	30
United Kingdom	28
Argentina	26
Norway	21
Spain	19
Netherlands	18
Belgium	17
Sweden	13
Venezuela	11
Hong Kong	9
Finland	8
Ecuador	8
Singapore	7
Canada	6
Luxembourg	5
Greece	5
Mexico	5
Ireland	2
Liechtenstein	2

Source: Society for Worldwide Interbank Financial
Telecommunications, 15 February 1980.

Messages can be transfers, foreign exchanges, and special messages, as listed in table 3-5, and must be in standardized form. For each type of message, the format defines the fields permissable; field content must also be in standarized form. (See table 3-6.) Messages can then be checked automatically for errors in the format or the standardized portions of the content. Security procedures include passwords, levels of access, and data encryption.

Messages can be delivered simultaneously to as many as ten addresses or to as many as twenty destinations with one group address. Online message retrieval is also possible for a limited time. Messages that have been sent within the previous two days can be retrieved in a matter of seconds. Messages between two and ten days old are also retrievable but require somewhat more time to find because they are stored offline. During normal operation, it may take up to ten minutes for a message to be delivered within the international network, unless the message is flagged as urgent. In that event, the message would be delivered within a minute. SWIFT can be accessed through computer terminals, main computers, or telex machines, although, even for low volume, telex is not considered as cost efficient as a computer terminal.

A number of companies market interface devices for national networks and for SWIFT. For example, Arbat Systems Ltd., a subsidiary of Arbuthnot Latham (the holding company for a London merchant bank), produces banking software for international bank accounting, money market trading, foreign exchange, and interfaces for SWIFT, CHIPS, and CHAPS (the latter a proposed network for banks in England). The company's systems are used by banks in the United States and Western Europe.

Table 3-5
Message Categories on the SWIFT Network

Message Category	Items in Category
Foreign exchange	Foreign exchange Fixed loan or deposit Call or notice of loan or deposit Interest payment
Bank transfers	Bank transfers Advice to receive
Customer transfers	
Special messages	Confirmation of debit Confirmation of credit Statements

Source: Based on the Society for Worldwide Interbank Financial Telecommunication's *General Information*, January 1978, p. 3.

Table 3-6
Sample Fields and Field Content in a SWIFT Message

Field Code[a]	Field Content[b]	Explanation
BNORBEBB200456		Terminal address, input sequence number
100		Message type
CYBAGB21		Bank code
20:	13562	Transaction reference number
32A:	791002USD600000	Date, currency code, and amount
50:	THORN J.	Customer's name
	AVE. DE L'OISEAU 35	Customer's address
	B-1001 BRUSSELS	
53D:	GUARANTY BANK	Correspondent bank of
	WALL STREET 306	the customer's bank
	NEW YORK 10080	
59:	/36281726	
	CLARKE K.	Recipient of the money
	HIGH STREET 40	
	LONDON EC3R 3AJ	
70:	INVOICE NO 3544 DATED	Additional details
	1979-10-02	

Source: Based on the Society for Worldwide Interbank Financial Telecommunication's *General Information*, January 1978, p. 5.

[a]Where applicable.

[b]In this example, J. Thorn wishes to have $600,000 in U.S. currency transferred to the account of K. Clarke.

Private Networks

Most of the largest banks also have extensive telecommunications networks joining their own foreign offices and branches, and groups of affiliated banks may have regional networks such as the data processing network operated by Western Bancorp, an affiliation of twenty-two banks with over eight hundred branches (and four thousand teller terminals) in eleven states in the western United States.

Citibank, one of the U.S. leaders in bank technology development, maintains a private leased-line telecommunications network with a main switching center in New York and other switching centers in London, Hong Kong, and Manama (Bahrain). Some eighty banks in sixty-five countries are interconnected; monthly volume in 1977 was over 325,000 transmissions.[49] About 90 percent of all the bank's telegraphic traffic and about 63 percent of all its telephone traffic flows through the network at some point. More recently, Citibank has been developing an electronic mail system to handle international loan syndication activities. Text processors are used to create and edit the letters describing the terms and conditions of the loans. These processors are connected through a microcomputer to the bank's telex system, and telex names and addresses are automatically supplied from a database that is stored, not on an inhouse computer, but on the General Electric timesharing network.

Bank of America, another leader in bank technology, has connected word processing systems directly, that is, not through the telex network. Eventually, Bank of America expects that bank managers on five continents will be electronically exchanging memoranda and letters of credit through the interconnected word processors. The bank currently leases over 130 circuits between New York and San Francisco, plus other leased lines to over eighty locations in Latin America for telegraph, voice, facsimile, or a combination. All told, the bank has branches or offices in about one hundred countries tied into the leased-line network, with about half the circuits used for computer data transmission.[50] In 1975, data transmission by the Bank of America across national borders totaled approximately 360 million bytes daily.

Other banks whose international operations may be somewhat smaller nonetheless use a mixture of leased lines, SWIFT, and dial-up access for computer data transmission and other electronic communication. For example, Wells Fargo Bank, with headquarters in San Francisco, has three private leased lines to New York, and full duplex leased lines between New York and London, New York and Hong Kong, and New York and Sao Paulo. Other telex lines join Tokyo, Seoul, and Singapore to Hong Kong, and Luxembourg to London. Computer data are transmitted weekly from London to San Francisco using dial access. In addition, the bank shares a leased line with several other banks to the SWIFT concentrator in New Jersey and leases a voice grade "hotline" (a service of Western Union) between San Francisco and New York so that as soon as the hotline telephone is picked up in one city, the telephone rings in the other city.

Bankers are also users of commercial timesharing services for data storage, computing power, software packages and databases, and digital transmission. Virtually hundreds of banks take part in some sort of data network, such as Tymnet, Telenet, General Electric's Mark III, National Data Corporation, and Rapidata.[51] The Mark III network, for example, which first offered timesharing services internationally in 1970, was serving over five thousand companies in twenty-two countries in 1978, and many of those companies are banks. As another example, Tymshare Inc., the operator of Tymnet, provides services and software to over one thousand banks. The OECD's survey of data networks in Europe questioned five computer timesharing bureaus, and two listed banks and financial institutions as their major customers.[52]

The provision of public or semipublic databases is also a feature of timesharing networks, whether the producer of the database is the network, a bank, a government agency, or some other organization. For instance, the I.P. Sharp timesharing service, a Canadian company, provides databases produced by the Bank of Canada, the International Monetary Fund, and the U.S. National Bureau of Economic Research. A listing of databases on another network, Telenet, contains at least a dozen distinctly banking databases in addition to fifty or sixty others for stocks and bonds, corporate financial information, gross economic data, and so on. (See table 3-7.)

Structural Effects

Generally, banks have been decentralizing their information systems as part of a wider trend in business practices. In data processing, the decentralization trend—or at least a move away from large centralized systems—has been wide-spread in recent years. According to one industry observer, the 1960s were dominated by large centralized computer systems, but in the 1970s costs and other economic factors encouraged distributed processing, and in the 1980s yet another pattern will emerge based on sharing computer resources through standard means for interconnecting dissimilar machines.[53] As early as 1972 a survey of computer equipment manufacturers confirmed an overall trend toward distributed data processing.[54] In a 1978 survey of distributed process-ing in 150 banks, 42 percent were using distributed processing techniques, and about 80 percent expected to be doing so eventually if not already.[55] According to a banking newspaper, many international banks decentralized both their management structures and their data processing systems in an

Table 3-7
Databases Related to Banking, Available on the Telenet Network

Database	Supplier
Bancall	FDIC
Bancompare	ADP Network Services
Banking	Canadian Department of Finance
Chartered Banks	Canadian Department of Finance
Citidata	Citibank
Currency	I.P. Sharp
FDIC Reports of Conditions	U.S. Federal Reserve Board
Flow of Funds	U.S. Federal Reserve Board
FX (foreign exchange)	ContiCurrency
IMS	International Monetary Fund
NBER Data Bank	National Bureau of Economic Research
OECD	Organization for Economic Cooperation and Development
OECDNIA	Organization for Economic Cooperation and Development
UKSCO	U.K. Central Statistics Office

Compiled from Telenet Communications Corporation's *Directory of Computer Based Services*, Vienna, Virg., 1979.

effort to improve service.[56] The authors of the OECD survey of data networks in Europe concluded that international networks were facilitating the practice of more decentralized decision making and management.[57] Thus for a variety of reasons, not the least of which are economic and legal, there seems to have been a shift toward more shared data processing in multinational banking in recent years. Whether there has been a similar increase in more shared decision making is less apparent.

Probably the most pervasive, and most obvious, effect on operations has been the standardization that has been agreed on. The banks in the CHIPS network, for example, agreed to use standardized names and addresses and universal five-digit identification codes for nearly five thousand international accounts. SWIFT, particularly, has been responsible for standardizing formats for funds transfer messages and other international banking functions. This standardization will be explored further in the next two chapters as one of the major determinants in interorganization relations.

There are a number of structural changes, or potential changes, in the banking industry that have been attributed to the use of SWIFT specifically. A study by Trolle-Schultz concludes that although SWIFT is not significantly faster than telex and is only marginally used in relation to worldwide payments traffic, it might well enable smaller banks to compete with the leading multinational banks.[58] Use of the network might also cause a gradual reduction in the amount of money in the international float (the money that has been debited at one location but has yet to be credited at another location) thus inclining the banking industry to use transaction fees to make up for lost income. And use of the SWIFT network might also increase the number of fluctuations in exchange rates but at the same time decrease the average amplitude of the fluctuations. The standardized SWIFT message, Trolle-Schultz suggests, is gradually replacing the draft, the mail transfer, and the cable transfer for international monetary transactions. Within a few years, corporate customers may themselves start using SWIFT standards to prepare payment messages before routing the messages electronically to the bank.

It has also been suggested that SWIFT may alter existing correspondent banking relationships, since a large network of personal correspondent relationships would be less necessary.[59] In the same way, foreign branches of larger banks may gain near autonomy in foreign payments, if permitted by the home office, by virtue of using the network directly instead of routing payments through the home office. Another perhaps noteworthy change seems to be the addition of more regional banks to the SWIFT network, at least in the United States; previously the U.S. members of SWIFT were the large money center banks, but lately the membership has expanded to include regional banks.[60]

Another outcome of SWIFT's growth has been multinational agreements on legal procedures. The SWIFT organization has prepared a comprehensive written policy defining who is legally liable for interest losses under given conditions, that is, whether the sending bank, the receiving bank, or SWIFT is responsible when an error on the network causes a message to go awry.[61]

On another front, shared networks and automated clearing centers in domestic retail banking have been credited with offering such benefits as decreased costs and increased convenience and security.[62] This is perhaps even more true for Western Europe, where automated clearing centers are more advanced than the clearing-center systems in the United States and are becoming a significant part of the entire money-moving mechanism. Eventually, according to a U.S. government report, the automated clearing systems will facilitate international transactions and may intensify the flow of funds among countries as well as increase the interdependence of monetary policies, which in turn might lead to coordination of banking supervisory policies.[63]

The decreasing autonomy of any country's domestic monetary policies has been remarked by numerous observers.[64] There are implications for money itself. A prediction made in 1965 that by 1990 or 1995 banking will be essentially a vast international electronic information system seems to be coming true.[65] If so, according to another source, current concepts about the velocity of money and the demand for money will become outdated, as money itself becomes something different.[66]

In short, international banking is one of the predominant institutions in world affairs, and multinational computer/telecommunications networks in banking are becoming more important than ever.[67] Structural changes in the world monetary system, in international banking, and in domestic banking have been attributed to or associated with the rise of transnational flows of information via telecommunications.

It is very difficult, however, to ascribe specific cause-and-effect relationships. It is more useful to recognize the interrelationships and the congruence of events and technologies that have encouraged us to produce the systems we have. On that ground we can then explore the specific dimensions of those relationships.

Notes

1. Sidney H. Aronson, "Bell's Electrical Toy: What's the Use?" in *The Social Impact of the Telephone*, ed. Ithiel de Sola Pool (Cambridge, Mass.: MIT Press, 1977), pp. 15-39.

2. *The Usage of International Data Networks in Europe* (Organization for Economic Cooperation and Development, 1979), pp. 209-218.

3. Ibid., pp. 198-208.

4. See, for example, Robert E. Jackson, "The Hidden Issues: What Kind of Order," *Journal of Communication* 29 (Summer 1979): 152-153.

5. "The Two Worlds of Banking and EDP," *Datamation*, July 1965, p. 23.

6. Robert S. Aldom, Alan B. Purdy, Robert T. Schneider, and Harry E. Whittingham, Jr., *Automation in Banking* (New Brunswick, N.J.: Rutgers University Press, 1963), pp. 13-15.

7. Boris Yavitz, *Automation in Commercial Banking* (New York: Columbia University and the Free Press, 1967), pp. 28-29.

8. Robert B. Forest, "Of Bankers and Computers," *Datamation*, April 1965, pp. 107-109.

9. Robert S. Aldom et al., *Automation in Banking* (New Brunswick, N.J.: Rutgers University Press, 1963), p. 172.

10. Boris Yavitz, *Automation in Commercial Banking* (New York: Columbia University and the Free Press, 1967), pp. 1, 79.

11. Ibid., p. 131.

12. James Vaughan and Avner Porat, *Banking Computer Style* (Englewood Cliffs, N.J.: Prentice-Hall, 1969).

13. Ibid., p. 87.

14. Ibid., p. 89.

15. Frank J. Fabozzi, ed., *The Impact of the Computer on Commercial Banking* (Hempstead, N.Y.: Hofstra University Press, 1975).

16. Robert J. Heldt, "An Overview of the Impact of Automation on Various Aspects of Commercial Banking," in Fabozzi, *Impact of Computer*, pp. 1-13.

17. John Roberts, "The Impact of Computers on Organizational Structure in Commercial Banks," in Fabozzi, *Impact of Computer*, pp. 84-108.

18. Paul Rossi, "The Impact of the Computer on Internal Operations of Commercial Banks," in Fabozzi, *Impact of Computer*, pp. 194-216.

19. Edith Myers, "EFT: Despite the Hurdles—Growth," *Datamation*, July 1978, pp. 187-188.

20. Jeffrey Kutler, "FDIC Finds EFT Has Not Meant Big Bank Domination," *American Banker*, 30 October 1979, pp. 1, 22.

21. Toni Wiseman, "Bank Terminals to Double by 1981: CSI," *Computerworld*, 3 October 1977, pp. 49-50.

22. Jeffrey Kutler, "Ultimate Growth of Home Banking Awaits Resolution of Legal, Technical Issues," *American Banker*, 24 January 1979, pp. 8-9.

23. "World ATMs Seen Reaching 246,819 by '85, 10 Times '78 Total," *American Banker*, 29 August 1979, p. 2.

24. "DP Costs Rising 12 Per Cent." *Bank Systems and Equipment*, November 1978, p. 66.

25. "IDC Cuts Database Down to Size to Boost Revenues and Usefulness," *Online Database Report*, June 1979, p. 1.

26. Bruce W. Hasenyager, "Automating the Office" (Paper presented at the 1978 Annual Conference, Association for Computing Machinery, Washington, D.C. December 4-6, 1978).

27. See William Musgrave, "The Computerized Work Station," *Dun's*

Review, July 1978, pp. 109-111; and Jeffrey Kutler, "Through Acquisition, Citibank NA Becomes Developer and Vendor of Office Automation," *American Banker,* 21 November 1979, pp. 6-7.

28. Howard A. Karten, "Automation Gives Bank Office New Look," *Computerworld*, 11 June 1979, p. 71.

29. Robert Rowthorn, *International Big Business 1957-1967* (Cambridge: Cambridge University Press, 1971), p. 1.

30. David A. Heenan and Warren J. Keegan, "The Rise of Third World Multinationals," *Harvard Business Review* 57 (January-February 1979): 101-109.

31. Ibid.

32. Center for Medieval and Renaissance Studies, *The Dawn of Modern Banking* (New York: Yale University Press, 1979), p. 106.

33. Stuart W. Robinson, Jr., *Multinational Banking* (Leiden: A.W. Sijthoff, 1969), p. 9.

34. In Howe Martyn, *Multinational Business Management* (Lexington, Mass.: Lexington Books, D.C. Heath, 1970), pp. 83-85.

35. James C. Baker and M. Gerald Bradford, *American Banks Abroad* (New York: Praeger, 1974), p. 9.

36. "Heimann Calls the Shots for Overseas Lending," *The Economist*, 14 January 1978, pp. 99-100.

37. Francis A. Lees, *Foreign Banking and Investment in the United States* (New York: John Wiley and Sons, 1976), p. 9.

38. Ibid., pp. 11-12.

39. Lawrence Rout, "Bank Invasion," *Wall Street Journal,* 24 November 1978, p. 1.

40. Fred H. Klopstock, "Foreign Banks in the United States: Scope and Growth of Operations" (Research Paper no. 7316, Federal Reserve Bank of New York, 1973).

41. U.S. Department of Commerce, *Foreign Direct Investment in the United States,* Report of the Secretary of Commerce to the Congress in Compliance with the Foreign Investment Study Act of 1974 (Washington, D.C.: U.S. Government Printing Office, 1976), pp. 106-107.

42. Francis A. Lees, *Foreign Banking and Investment in the United States* (New York: John Wiley and Sons, 1976), p. 50.

43. "Foreign Banks Unlikely to Exert Undue Control in U.S. Market, PSI Study Says," *American Banker*, 3 November 1979, pp. 2, 7.

44. Stuart W. Robinson, Jr., *Multinational Banking* (Leiden: A.W. Sijthoff, 1969), p. 8.

45. Martin Mayer, *The Bankers* (New York: Weybright and Talley, 1974), pp. 460-462.

46. See, for example, Genie Short and Betsy White, "International Bank Lending: A Guided Tour through the Data," *Federal Reserve Bank of New York Quarterly Review*, Autumn 1978, pp. 39-46.

47. "Two CHIPS Members Link Computers with Machines at New York CHA," *American Banker*, 11 April 1979, pp. 2, 12.

48. Jeffrey Kutler, "SWIFT Codifies Liabilities," *American Banker*, 18 June 1979, pp. 1, 22.

49. Robert B. White, "Prepared Statement," *Hearings before the Subcommittee on International Operations of the Committee on Foreign Relations*, U.S. Senate, 95th Cong., 1st sess., 8-10 June 1977, pp. 252-254.

50. Jeffrey Kutler, "Spread of Transborder Data Flow Laws Compounds Intl. Operations Challenge," *American Banker*, 7 March 1979, p. 8.

51. "Bank Talk Is Far from Cheap," *Bank Systems and Equipment*, April 1978, pp. 61-62.

52. *The Usage of Data Networks in Europe* (Paris: Organization for Economic Cooperation and Development, 1979).

53. Tim Scannell, "Lecht Voices Fears for Users' Survival in 1980s," *Computerworld*, 11 June 1979, p. 7.

54. D.J. Theis, "Communication Processors," *Datamation*, August 1972, pp. 321-344.

55. Alan Richman, "8 of 10 Banks/Thrifts Will Use Distributed Systems Eventually," *Bank Systems and Equipment*, July 1978, pp. 32-37.

56. Jeffrey Kutler, "Word Processing Technology ahead of Most Banks' Abilities to Use It," *American Banker*, 3 June 1979, p. 8.

57. *The Usage of Data Networks in Europe* (Paris: Organization for Economic Cooperation and Development, 1979), p. 11.

58. Erik Trolle-Schultz, "International Money Transfer Developments," *Journal of Bank Research* 9 (Summer 1978): 73-77.

59. Margaret Thoren, "The Prime Mover at SWIFT: An Interview with Carl Reuterskiold," *Banker's Magazine,* September 1978, pp. 35-36.

60. Jeffrey Kutler, "SWIFT Codifies Liabilities," *American Banker,* 18 June 1979, pp. 1, 22.

61. Ibid.

62. National Commission on Electronic Fund Transfers, *EFT in the United States* (Washington, D.C.: U.S. Government Printing Office, 1970), pp. 222-234.

63. Ibid.

64. See, for example: Robert J. Carbaugh and Fan Liang-Shing, *The International Monetary System* (Lawrence, Kans.: University of Kansas Press, 1976); William Ellington, "U.S. Banks Are Losing Their Dominance in Eurocurrency Lending," *Wall Street Journal*, 14 December 1978, p. 18; Francis A. Lees, *Foreign Banking and Investment in the United States* (New York: John Wiley and Sons, 1976); Robert Rowthorn, *International Big Business 1957-1967* (Cambridge: Cambridge University Press, 1971).

65. Martin Greenberger, quoted in Robert B. Forest, "Of Bankers and Computers," *Datamation*, April 1965, pp. 107-109.

66. George Garvey and Martin R. Blyn, *The Velocity of Money* (New York: Federal Reserve Bank of New York, 1969), p. 84.

67. Anthony Oettinger et al., *High and Low Politics: Information Resources for the 80s* (Cambridge, Mass.: Ballinger, 1977), p. xiv.

4

A Survey of the Largest Banks

In interorganization relations research, the unit of analysis is the network as a whole, and determinants or dimensions are established to both describe and explain the interrelationships. Four key concepts in such analyses are formalization, intensity, reciprocity, and standardization. With these four dimensions as a guide, a survey was conducted among the largest commercial banks regarding their relationships via telecommunications and computer networks. The following chapter presents the results of that survey. In chapter 5 these results will be evaluated within a broader, more historical context.

Major Dimensions

During the past thirty years, social scientists have developed various ways of seeing structure in interorganization relationships. Marrett reported in 1971 that there appeared to be some convergence of interests and terminology in the series of studies, dating back to at least 1951, which she reviewed and summarized.[1] The four dimensions outlined by Marrett—formalization, intensity, reciprocity, standardization—are used here as the means of organizing this inquiry. The definitions and explanations given here are based largely on Marrett and on a later textbook by Aldrich, athough, of course, these are not the only determinants and dimensions that have been proposed for interorganization research.[2] In specific areas of investigation some concepts are more appropriate than others, and the Marrett-Aldrich concepts seem most useful here.

Formalization is the degree to which official sanction is given to the interorganization relationships. According to Marrett, there are two useful measures of formalization: agreement formalization and structural formalization. The first measure refers to the official recognition and approval of the relations. The second measure refers to the extent to which an intermediary organization coordinates the relationships among the organizations under study.

As Aldrich points out, traditional theories of bureaucratic organization emphasize the importance of formalization, especially as an agent of stabilization and continuity. The same is true, he says, for interorganization relations. Structural formalization is of particular importance in societies where the state's role is significant. Regulatory agencies, government programs, and other governmental and quasi-governmental bodies impose conditions on the types and conduct of relationships among organizations.

Intensity is a companion measure to formalization, designed to address the problem of varying levels of involvement in or commitment to the interorganization relations. Marrett distinguishes two indicators of intensity: the size of the resource investment and the frequency of interaction. Measurement of the resource investment may be as simple as the cost in dollars of maintaining the relationship. Or the measurement might involve counting the number of services one organization provides another or evaluating the nature of the interaction. In addition, the level at which interaction takes place within the organization also may be evaluated. Contacts at higher levels might be much more influential than contacts at lower organizational levels.

Reciprocity refers to a balance or symmetry in the relationships. Generally, it is much easier to discuss reciprocity when the relationship is between two organizations rather than among many. The central concern, in both Marrett and Aldrich, is with the distribution of power, the power balance, between two organizations. Thus reciprocity has been divided into two parts: resource reciprocity—that is, the flow or exchange of resources or elements, and definitional reciprocity—the extent to which the conditions of the exchange were agreed on mutually. When many organizations are involved with multiple ties, the assessment of reciprocity is considerably more difficult.

In the context of telecommunications networks and computer databases, an indication of resource reciprocity might be the symmetry, or asymmetry, of access to computerized information banks or databases. This emphasis on information as a resource is based in part on organization theorists' respect for the role of information processing in maintaining an organization. Herbert Simon, in *The New Science of Management Decision*, points out that the exercise of authority is one of the most pervasive phenomena in organizations and that authority is exercised when a person accepts decision premises provided by another or by a computer.[3] If there is a common set of databases used by the major international banks, for example, then it might be reasonable to conclude that there is a set of shared decision premises within the cluster of organizations. (Since a premise is a previous statement or assertion used as the basis for an argument, the "facts" in a database can under some conditions be considered as decision premises provided by a computer.) Alternately, the patterns of access or use of a given set of databases might indicate the power balance among the organizations, although not necessarily indicating any organization's power over the activities of specific other organizations in the group.

Finally, *standardization*, the fourth dimension or determinant, is a traditional notion in organization theory and quite likely an inevitable result of formalized transactions among organizations. Standardization, like the other three dimensions, is divided into two subsets: standardization of the unit of exchange and standardization of procedures for exchange. Standardization is not the same as formalization, Marrett argues, because the formalized arrange-ment may not be detailed or explicit regarding the units and process of exchange. At the same time, standardization is more likely to be found in formalized relationships than in nonformalized ones. Positive correlations have been found between standardization and organizational size and complexity and with intensity of interaction. Aldrich suggests that standard procedures, because of either inherent or implied efficiences, are favored in the business community. Marrett, though, chose to sidestep the arguments over efficiency or effectiveness and presented degree of standardization as a measure without intending to evaluate the results of standardization.

The Survey

During late 1979, an attempt was made to measure the interorganization rela-tions among banks in terms of contact via computer/telecommunications, using the four dimensions as the basis for framing the questions. The purpose of the survey was to collect data that would describe the extent of telecommuni-cations-based interaction at the present time. The survey would also provide part of the material for the broader, more historical assessment in the next chapter.

A questionnaire, or "checklist" as it was called, was designed, tested, and sent to some of the largest commercial banks in the world. The banks were chosen from several published lists of the largest banks, since the lists do vary slightly depending on date of publication and criteria for ranking.[4] As the previous chapters have indicated, the larger commercial banks preceded the medium and small banks in using computers, in using networks, and in engag-ing in international banking. The choice of the fifty largest was also influenced by the desire to have a sample consisting of organizations fairly similar in size, complexity, activities, and scope of operations.

Questionnaires were sent to 248 officers at the fifty institutions—in the great majority of the cases five questionnaires per organization. To the extent possible, each questionnaire was personally addressed to the head of economic research, the head of foreign exchange activities, the head of international lending, and the general managers of the organization's New York and London branches. These were selected as the most likely areas where commercial data-bases might be used (for example, in economic research and perhaps foreign exchange), where computer networks might be used (for example, in foreign exchange and perhaps in international lending), and where interorganization telecommunications might be greatest (for example, at the money center branches such as New York and London). Of course some exceptions had to be made in addressing the questionnaires. Not all the banks have London and New York branches; some banks in fact have their headquarters in those cities. And not all the banks in the sample provide in published directories personal names or titles equivalent to the categories selected.

Finally, it must be emphasized that the results given in this chapter are primarily based on personal estimates of participants (although presumably they are informed estimates). Several bankers wrote that the diversity and complexity of their operations prevented complete accuracy, and several also wrote that to answer the questions fully would require extensive surveys on their own part and an immense amount of research on their own operations. On the other hand, at least one bank did organize an effort to respond completely, apparently requiring the heads of all the bank's major departments to each complete a copy of the questionnaire.

Profile of Participants

Responses were received from forty-nine of the fifty organizations (all the countries), or, to put it differently, from 140 of the individuals (56 percent). The one bank that did not respond probably should not have been included in the first place, since it is more similar to a savings bank in the United States than to a commercial bank, and it had no branches in New York or London at the time of the survey. Since some of the participants combined their answers with those of other people in their organizations, and some noted that company policy prevented their answering either in whole or in part, the number of usable responses was 123, or 50 percent.

A profile of the participants is provided in figures 4-1 and 4-2. The organizations represented had assets ranging from $20 billion to $95 billion and employed from 3,000 to an estimated 90,000 persons, with the bulk of the organizations employing about 20,000. Respondents living in English speaking countries (Canada, the United States, and the United Kingdom) accounted for just under half of the sample. This includes the responses from foreign branches in London and New York. Looking at the respondents by area of residence, the London group formed the single greatest concentration; 80 percent of the 59 questionnaires sent to London were returned. Participants from banks with home offices in Japan accounted for the largest single group by country, which follows from the fact that Japanese banks are the largest single group in the top fifty commercial banks. When categorized into only three major geographical areas based on the country of the home office, the largest group was formed by respondents with home offices in Western Europe (48.8 percent), followed by North America (28.5 percent), and then Japan (22.8 percent). To protect the confidentiality of the responses, all further breakdowns by country will be limited to those three general groups, that is, Japan, North America (the United States and Canada), and Western Europe (plus Brazil). Otherwise the corporate identity of some of the respondents

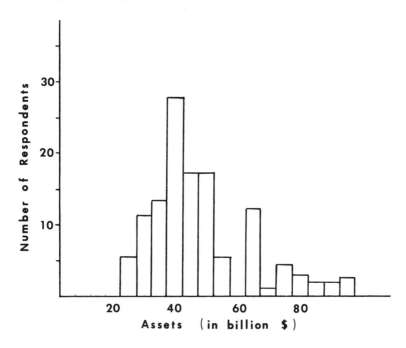

Figure 4-1. Assets of Respondents' Parent Organizations (N=123)

might be obvious because of the small number of banks selected from certain countries. However, a list of all the countries included in the survey is incorporated into table 4-1.

Grouping the respondents by their major activity reveals that many are engaged in international lending. Slightly less than half (sixty-one) indicated that a major activity of their department was international lending, fifty-one checked "foreign exchange," and fourteen checked "economic research." (See table 4-2.) One banker noted that, for his institution, foreign exchange and international lending are highly interrelated; this was apparently true for at least thirty-six other respondents who checked both categories as major activities for their departments. The diversity of departments responding, despite the attempt to limit the survey to a small set of banking activities, can be demonstrated by listing some of the major activities voluntarily written in by respondents: general administration, communications (2), organization and EDP, controller, domestic international banking, international banking (2), international stocks, international commercial business, foreign department, correspondent relations, foreign business promotion, new issues and syndication, commercial loans, commercial customers, money market (2), money transfer, payment orders, international payments, collections and

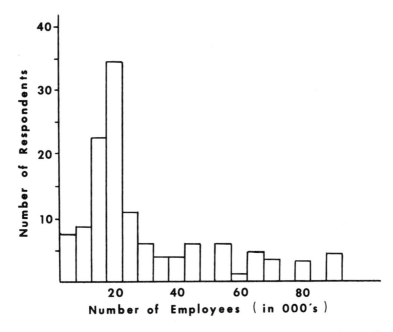

Figure 4-2. Number of Employees in Parent Organizations (*N*=123)

documentary credits, paying and receiving, export/import, bullion, funds operation, fund dealing, and local finance.

Results

Two questions in the survey pertained to formalization, and the responses indicated a high degree of such formalization. In the first instance, a type of

Table 4-1
Geographic Distribution of Respondents, by Location of Home Office (*N*=123)

	Home Office	Foreign Office or Branch	Total
Japan	12	16	28
North America	21	14	35
Western Europe	33	27	60

Note: The participating countries and their representation in the total sample are: Belgium (2.4 percent); Brazil (2.4 percent); Canada (8.9 percent); France (4.1 percent); Italy (3.3 percent); Japan (22.8 percent); The Netherlands (8.9 percent); Switzerland (5.7 percent); United Kingdom (9.8 percent); United States (19.5 percent); and West Germany (12.2 percent).

Table 4-2
Major Activities of Respondents

	Home Office	Foreign Office or Branch	Total
International loans	31	30	61
Foreign exchange	29	22	51
Economic research	13	1	14
Other	14	24	40

Note: The total is greater than 123 because multiple answers were possible; respondents checking both international loans and foreign exchange have been included on both lines, for example.

agreement formalization is the syndicated loan, where groups of banks take part in backing large loans with one bank serving as the lead bank. In response to a question on increasing involvement in internationally syndicated loans, 85 percent of the respondents agreed that their own banks were in fact becoming increasingly involved. (See table 4-3.) Only 6 of the 123 respondents disagreed with the statement. One person objected to the word "increasing," since his bank was already, he said, heavily involved.

A second question was aimed at a specific area of possible structural formalization by attempting to measure the influence of SWIFT. The question asked whether or not the respondent's bank was using SWIFT message formats (or SWIFT-like formats) for transactions even when the SWIFT network itself would not be used. This is admittedly an oblique indication of structural formalization, but it would suggest the pervasiveness of the intermediary's influence, that is, a coordinating side effect of using the SWIFT network. Approximately 46 percent said that their bank was not using SWIFT formats in non-SWIFT applications, and 35 percent said that they were. The remaining 19 percent did not know or declined to say. Respondents from home offices tended to be split on that question while respondents from foreign branches or offices tended to disagree. (See table 4-4.) A possible explanation is that respondents at home offices are more aware of activity within the organization to adapt to SWIFT,

Table 4-3
Involvement in Internationally Syndicated Loans (N=123)

	Agree			Uncertain		Disagree	
Our bank is increasingly involved in internationally syndicated credits or loans.	59	43	3	12	2	3	1

Table 4-4

Use of SWIFT or SWIFT-like Formats in Non-SWIFT Applications (N=123)

Does your bank use SWIFT or SWIFT-like formats for messages or transactions even when the message or transaction is not to be transmitted via SWIFT?

	Home			Branch		
	Yes	No	Uncertain	Yes	No	Uncertain
Japan	4	5	3	2	12	2
North America	9	4	8	8	5	1
Western Europe	13	12	8	7	18	2
Totals	26	21	18	17	35	5

but such adaptations have yet to be substantially felt at the branch offices. Conversely, the apparent difference in opinion may result from the simple fact that branch officers were answering with respect to a much more restricted area of operations. A look at a breakdown by country of home office seems to show that the North American home-office group was relatively more in agreement (if the "uncertain" group can be ignored) than any other subgroup, although the cell sizes are extremely small. (See table 4-4.)

The survey contained two sections measuring the second type of intensity, that is, the frequency of interaction. The first question asked for estimates of the amount of time—as a percentage of the normal working day—spent in telecommunications contact with other banks. The second question asked each participant to estimate the frequency of telecommunications-based contact with each other bank in the survey.

The older forms of telecommunications (telephone and telex) received the highest estimates for use in interbank exchanges. Overall, respondents estimated that during an average working day their departments were in contact with other banks about 34 percent of the day via telephone conversations, about 32 percent of the day via telex, 9 percent of the day via computer networks, and about 4 percent of the day using facsimile. However, estimates ranged in all categories from 0 to 100 percent of the day. (See table 4-5.) The estimations did not have to be mutually exclusive; respondents could have estimated use of all four forms of telecommunications at 100 percent of the average day.

An earlier survey among international bankers in New York City produced similar results. In that survey, telex was rated as the most important telecommunications medium for daily international banking operations, followed closely in importance by the telephone; however, by 1985 it was almost unanimously agreed that computer networks would be the most important medium for interbank exchanges.[5]

Table 4-5
Overall Use of Telecommunications to Contact Other Banks (N=110)

	0	1-10	20	30	40	50	60	70	80	90	100	Mean Percentage	Standard Deviation
Telephone	2	38	17	1	7	6	7	7	5	3	7	33.7	30.5
Telex	6	42	11	13	7	9	4	1	2	3	12	32.1	32.0
Computer net	67	26	6	2	–	–	1	–	–	–	6	9.1	23.4
Facsimile	72	34	–	–	2	1	–	–	–	–	1	3.7	11.9

Percentage of Average Day

Note: Respondents not answering the question have been excluded. Cell counts are the numbers of respondents giving estimates within the range indicated.

It appears as if participants from home offices estimated greater time spent using telex and computer networks and less time on the telephone than did participants at foreign offices or branches. (See table 4-6.) But the difference may not be substantial, since it fails to be statistically significant using analysis of variance. (The use of a statistical test is mentioned only for comparison purposes, since basic assumptions governing the use of the test, such as random sampling, do not apply here.)

Some larger differences did appear in the estimates when grouped by country of home office. Respondents from banks with home offices in North America estimated less use of both the telephone and telex for contacting other banks than did the other two geographical groups. (See table 4-6.) The European-based group, on the other hand, estimated more use of computer networks, on average, for interbank contacts than did the other two groups, but the numbers are much smaller and, again for comparison purposes, not statistically significant.

Table 4-6
Use of Telecommunications to Contact Other Banks, by Subgroup (N=110)

	Home		Branch		
	N	Mean Percent	N	Mean Percent	Group Means
Telephone					
Japan	11	16.18	16	51.88	37.33
North America	18	19.56	12	17.58	18.77
Western Europe	30	41.23	23	39.30	40.40
Group means		29.95		38.14	
Telex					
Japan	11	52.00	16	34.69	41.74
North America	18	21.39	12	16.92	19.60
Western Europe	30	36.70	23	31.09	34.26
Group means		34.88		28.88	
Computer network					
Japan	11	0.0	16	5.63	3.33
North America	18	9.11	12	2.17	6.30
Western Europe	30	17.50	23	31.09	13.53
Group means		11.68		6.04	
Facsimile					
Japan	11	1.82	16	7.50	5.19
North America	18	2.56	12	0.67	1.80
Western Europe	30	5.03	23	2.78	4.06
Group means		3.68		3.76	

Respondents checking foreign exchange as one of their major activities consistently estimated more time spent using all four of the telecommunications channels than did other categories based on activity. This, of course, would be expected, since foreign exchange is a volatile activity requiring constant and quick exchange of information.

A few respondents pointed out the difficulty of giving percentages for large departments. One person wrote that their department could not answer meaningfully if the answer was supposed to cover the entire staff. Another banker mentioned that activity is concentrated between 10 A.M. and 4 P.M. each day and that during that time there is always contact with international banks by telephone or telex. A London respondent advised that London banks still often rely on messenger service rather than the post or telephone.

On the specific question of contact via computer, only 36 percent of all respondents estimated that some department other than their own would probably be involved in a greater amount of interbank computer telecommunications. Some of the suggested other departments were: various regional offices; systems (3); computer department (2); operations (3); telex switching; management services; international treasury; international operations; international banking; international division; international finance; foreign department (2); letters of credit; money transfer; syndicated loans; foreign exchange; payments; domestic settlements; and credit.

The overall estimates are modified obviously by the responses from departments that do not engage in a lot of telecommunications contact with other banks, such as the economic research departments. However, the indication of this measure of intensity is that in telecommunications relationships the telephone and telex predominate and that computer network use is relatively quite small in terms of "time spent using" the facility, although not as small as facsimile. If the estimations are reliable, there also seems to be a greater use of computer networks by Western European banks than by Japanese or North American banks, at least in the areas of foreign exchange and international operations.

The second measure of the frequency of interaction was directed specifically at telecommunications contact with each other bank in the survey. Respondents were asked to estimate how often (daily, weekly, monthly, rarely, not at all) their own departments were in telecommunications contact with each of fifty given banks.

Generally, all the banks listed were reported to receive daily telecommunications contact from at least some of the other banks, although perhaps not from all the other banks. Slightly over one-third of all respondents reported daily or weekly telecommunications contact with all the fifty banks. About half of the respondents reported daily or weekly telecommunications contact with at least thirty of the fifty banks. (See table 4-7.)

Despite the fact that about half of the respondents were at either London

Table 4-7
Frequency of Telecommunications Contact among the Largest Commercial Banks (N=123)

	Daily	Weekly	Monthly	Rarely	None/No Answer
Morgan Guaranty Trust	62	21	8	17	15
Bank of America	57	26	4	21	15
Chase Manhattan	58	27	7	17	14
Bankers Trust	57	25	7	19	15
Manufacturers Hanover Trust	56	27	8	15	17
Citibank	57	24	5	18	19
Deutsche Bank	56	19	14	14	20
Chemical Bank	52	24	11	21	15
Midland Bank	52	21	15	17	18
Bank of Tokyo	47	28	14	16	18
Barclays Bank Ltd.	50	21	13	19	20
Barclays Bank International	50	21	14	19	19
National Westminster	51	19	17	16	20
Union Bank of Switzerland	51	15	17	19	21
Swiss Bank Corporation	52	15	15	20	21
Lloyds Bank Ltd.	47	23	13	18	22
Continental Illinois	44	23	17	23	16
Amsterdam-Rotterdam Bank	51	14	20	18	20
Dresdner Bank	47	19	16	19	22
Société Générale (Paris)	44	22	18	18	21
Crédit Lyonnais	42	23	21	17	20
Banque Nationale de Paris	47	20	15	20	21
Crédit Suisse	47	15	21	19	21
Algemene Bank Nederland	44	24	12	20	22
Royal Bank of Canada	39	26	17	21	20
Banca Commerciale Italiana	42	17	25	19	20
Société Générale de Banque	42	20	21	19	21
Bank of Montreal	39	22	23	19	20
Commerzbank	45	17	18	20	23
Dai-Ichi Kangyo Bank	33	32	17	24	17
Sumitomo Bank	31	31	22	21	18
Misubishi Bank	33	28	21	23	18
Fuji Bank	30	30	25	19	19
Toronto Dominion Bank	34	29	18	21	21
Mitsui Bank	31	30	20	24	18
Banca Nazionale del Lavoro	34	28	16	24	21

Table 4-7 *continued*

	Daily	Weekly	Monthly	Rarely	None/No Answer
Canadian Imperial Bank	30	30	20	22	21
Sanwa Bank	31	27	22	24	19
Westdeutsche Landesbank	36	22	17	25	23
Bank of Nova Scotia	34	22	20	26	21
Bayerische Landesbank	34	22	16	29	22
Bayerische Vereinsbank	34	22	16	27	24
Industrial Bank of Japan	26	28	20	27	22
Hypobank	31	22	11	35	24
Tokai Bank	25	28	19	28	23
Taiyo Kobe Bank	20	34	17	30	22
Banco do Brasil	22	29	18	30	24
Long-Term Credit Bank, Japan	20	32	16	34	21
Caisse Nationale de Crédit	27	18	16	38	24
Rabobank	22	23	16	35	27

Note: Ranking is approximate and does not include contact with one's own organization.

or New York branches of nonnative banks, there was vitually no difference between the responses of the home-office group and the foreign-office group. This was true for all banks but one (Bankers Trust was rated higher, that is, more frequent contact, by foreign branches than by home offices). On the other hand, there was a noticeable difference between the estimates from respondents whose departments are engaged in either foreign exchange or international lending and those whose departments are engaged in other activities. The former group estimated more frequent contact via telecommunications with almost all the fifty banks. The only banks for which this was not true were Hypobank, Sumitomo Bank, and Rabobank.

A few of the respondents mentioned some difficulty in estimating average contact with other banks, and some participants chose not to respond to this section at all. One wrote "no idea" across the section, and another said that, since the frequency depended on specific business, there could be no average frequency. A third participant added that during an average day their department dealt with about 10,000 telexes and innumerable telephone calls from other banks and that that could not be broken down further.

When asked if other departments in the bank might be in contact with the listed banks to a greater degree, some 46 percent said no and 42 percent said yes. Among the other departments listed as candidates for greater interbank contact were: international department or division (8); international banking (2); international operations; international business; international finance; foreign division (2); business operations; correspondent (4); banking and operations; trust; loan syndication (2); securities (2); commercial; financial; treasury; bond finance; documentary; computer division; paying and receiving; foreign exchange (7); money desk (2); transfer of funds; remittance; bullion; payment; traders; and money market (2).

Together, the two measures of intensity show frequent interaction via telecommunications, tempered by the type of departmental activity and perhaps by the nationality of the home office.

Two measures of reciprocity were contained in the survey, one aimed at detecting patterns of telecommunications relationships and the other directed toward detecting patterns of use of commercial databases.

The relationships based on estimated telecommunications contact showed a certain amount of imbalance. Given a list of fifty of the largest commercial banks (the same banks that comprised the survey population, table 4-7), respondents indicated that the most frequent telecommunications contact was with U.S. banks as a group, followed by U.K. banks, Swiss banks, and then the others. Using an approximate ranking procedure, which assigned a value of 0 to 4 for "no contact" to "daily contact," U.S. banks fill the top six positions, and U.S. and U.K. banks together fill ten of the top twelve positions (table 4-7). At the other end of the list, ten of the eleven Japanese banks in the survey are ranked in the bottom half. The exception is the Bank of Tokyo, ranked near the top.

A factor analysis was performed to look for large groups.[6] The principle components analysis of the estimated frequency of contact revealed almost clean divisions between U.S. banks, Japanese banks, and Western European banks (with Brazil and Canada in the latter group). (See table 4-8.) In a second attempt to test for large groupings of the estimated frequencies of contact, a clustering algorithm was used in which variables (the scores for each bank) were joined to clusters and clusters were successively joined to each other, until a single group encompasses all.[7] At each step, the two clusters with the minimum difference between their average correlations were joined. Again, three large groups were revealed; the eight U.S. banks clustered together, the eleven Japanese banks clustered together, and most of the Western European banks clustered together as a group and, within that, often by country. As figure 4-3 shows, each of the larger clusters encompasses a number of smaller clusters. Within the Western Europe-Canada cluster, five of the West German banks are grouped together, the five Canadian banks are grouped together, and the five U.K. banks are grouped together.

The second reciprocity measure, use of databases of economic information, resulted in relatively little support for the notion that a small group of the same databases of economic information might be used by all the banks in the sample. Instead, few of the thirty-one databases, which had been selected as the ones most likely to be used on the basis of published reports

Table 4-8

Major Groups of Banks Produced by Factor Analysis of Frequency of Contact

	Factor A	Factor B	Factor C
Banca Commerciale Italiana	0.835	–	–
Deutsche Bank	0.820	–	–
Crédit Suisse	0.818	–	–
Hypobank	0.814	–	–
Société Générale de Banque	0.805	–	–
Union Bank of Switzerland	0.804	–	–
Bank of Montreal	0.797	–	–
Swiss Bank Corporation	0.790	–	–
Commerzbank	0.786	–	–
Bayerische Landesbank Giro.	0.782	–	–
Amsterdam-Rotterdam Bank	0.776	–	–
Banca Nazionale del Lavoro	0.776	–	–
Bayerische Vereinsbank	0.772	–	–
Algemene Bank Nederland	0.772	–	–
Dresdner Bank	0.768	–	–
Westdeutsche Landesbank Giro.	0.764	–	–
Midland Bank	0.762	–	–
Canadian Imperial Bank of Com	0.758	–	–
Royal Bank of Canada	0.752	–	–
Banque Nationale de Paris	0.741	–	–
Toronto Dominion Bank	0.736	–	–
Barclays Bank Ltd.	0.734	–	–
Bank of Nova Scotia	0.733	–	–
Barclays Bank International	0.732	–	–
Société Générale (Paris)	0.730	–	–
Rabobank	0.725	–	–
Caisse Nationale de Crédit Agr	0.724	–	–
Lloyds Bank Ltd.	0.719	–	–
Banco do Brasil	0.713	–	–
National Westminster	0.694	–	–
Crédit Lyonnais	0.671	–	0.500
Taiyo Kobe Bank	–	0.844	–
Tokai Bank	–	0.840	–
Sanwa Bank	–	0.831	–
Industrial Bank of Japan	–	0.825	–
Mitsui Bank	–	0.811	–
Long-Term Credit Bank, Japan	–	0.810	–
Misubishi Bank	–	0.794	–

Table 4–8 *continued*

	Factor A	Factor B	Factor C
Sumitomo Bank	–	0.776	–
Dai-Ichi Kangyo Bank	–	0.760	–
Fuji Bank	–	0.731	–
Bank of Tokyo	–	0.695	–
Chase Manhattan	–	–	0.745
Bank of America	–	–	0.715
Citibank	0.542	–	0.704
Bankers Trust	–	–	0.691
Manufacturers Hanover	–	–	0.684
Chemical Bank	–	–	0.680
Morgan Guaranty Trust	–	–	0.667
Continental Illinois	0.544	–	0.581

Note: Factor loadings have been rotated and sorted; only values greater than 0.5 are shown; principle components: BMD P4M.

and correspondence with database producers and suppliers, were reportedly used by more than a handful of the respondents. Only about half (fifty-nine) of the respondents (representing thirty-five of the fifty banks) indicated that they used even one of the databases—whether daily, weekly, monthly, rarely, or never. (See table 4-9.)

The respondents who said that their departments did use any of the databases were roughly evenly divided between home offices and foreign offices (table 4-10). The greatest number of users from any single geographic area were from banks with home offices in Western Europe, but users from banks based in North America formed the greatest percentage of the group's representation in the total sample, that is, at least one database was reported used by 54 percent of the North American respondents, by 47 percent of the Western European respondents, and by 43 percent of the Japanese respondents.

None of the databases was said to be used by more than twenty-three respondents. About half of the listed databases were checked by a dozen or fewer respondents. Ranking the databases by frequency of use (4 = daily to 0 = never), the highest ranking database was Flow of Funds, produced by the U.S. Federal Reserve. Among the top ten were four databases produced by international groups (namely, by the World Bank and by the International Monetary Fund) and three produced by the U.S. Federal Reserve System.

In addition to the databases listed in the questionnaire, names of other databases or services were written in by about fifteen respondents. These databases were: Reuters (mentioned by three respondents); Telerate (mentioned

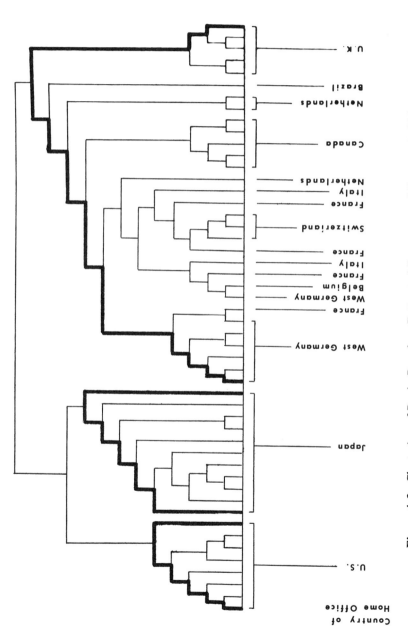

Figure 4-3. Clustering of Banks Based on Estimated Frequency of Contact via Telecommunications

Table 4-9
Estimated Frequency of Use of Commercial Databases (N=59)

Database (Producer)	Daily	Weekly	Monthly	Rarely	Never	Total Users
Flow of Funds (U.S. Federal Reserve)	7	6	3	6	37	22
Balance of Payments (Intl. Monetary Fund)	3	8	5	7	36	23
International Finance (Intl. Monetary Fund)	4	6	6	7	36	23
World Debt Tables (World Bank)	2	3	12	6	36	23
U.S. Weekly Banking (U.S. Federal Reserve)	2	10	3	3	41	18
Foreign Exchange (Chase Econometrics)	5	3	4	5	42	17
FRBSF (Federal Reserve Bank of San Francisco)	6	1	3	6	43	16
Merrill Lynch Economics (Merrill Lynch)	2	5	5	4	43	16
World Tables (World Bank)	2	1	9	6	41	18
Spot Rates–Currency (Extel Statistics)	5	1	2	6	45	14
BAI–Money Market (Bank of America)	5	4	–	1	49	10
OECD databanks (OECD)	2	3	5	5	44	15
Business Conditions (U.S. Dept. of Commerce)	2	3	6	2	46	13
BAB–Banks (Bank of America)	4	3	–	3	49	10
U.K. Central Statistics Office (U.K. govt.)	1	1	7	6	44	15
FDIC Reports (U.S. FDIC)	2	3	2	6	46	13
Eurabank (European American Bank)	2	1	4	6	46	13
Citidata (Citibank)	–	3	3	7	46	13
Compustat Bankfile (Standard & Poor)	–	3	3	6	47	12
Bank of Canada (Canadian Government)	–	3	2	3	51	8
Business International (Business Intl. Corp)	1	2	2	2	52	7

Chartered Banks (Canadian Government)	1	3	—	2	53	6
GE Economic Forecast (General Electric)	—	1	3	4	51	8
Money Market (CSC, Inc.)	1	2	—	3	53	6
Bonds (CSC, Inc.)	1	1	—	5	52	7
Currency Exchange (General Electric)	1	—	1	5	52	7
Industrial Bank of Japan	1	—	1	5	52	7
Interest Rate Futures (CIS)	—	1	2	3	53	8
Bancompare (ADP Network)	—	1	—	3	55	4
Currency (I.P. Sharp)	—	1	—	2	56	3
Bankanal (Robin-Humphrey)	—	—	—	4	55	4

Note: Other databases voluntarily listed by respondents were: Reuters; ADP databases; Telerate; Euromarkets Information; Caploan; Eurex; Data Resources; NEEDS-TS (Japan); Telekurs; Bank of England Statistics.

Table 4-10
Profile of Respondents Indicating Use of at Least One
Database (N=59)
(percent)

	Each Group's Representation in Total Sample
Home office	47 (31/66)
Foreign office/branch	49 (28/57)
Foreign exchange and international loans	46 (32/70)
Other activities	51 (27/53)
Japan	43 (12/28)
North America	54 (19/35)
Western Europe	47 (28/60)

by two respondents); ADP databases (mentioned by two respondents); Euro-markets Information System; Caploan; Eurex; Data Resources; Bank of England Statistical Tables; NEEDS-TS; Telekurs; and CHART, CHEMLINK, TRANSCEND, CASH CONNECTOR, and MARS. The latter group are cash management systems, which may include proprietary databases as well as public-ly available data.

Only one or two of the databases stood out as being used more by one group than another in the analysis by subgroups. When grouped by country of home office, very few differences appeared. The only exception was for the Eurabank database, which seems to stem from the fact that most of the users were from banks based in Europe and none was from a bank based in the United States. (Eurabank is a database of financial information for some twelve hundred non-U.S. banking organizations.) When the estimated frequencies of use were divided by departmental activity, again little difference appeared. Possible exceptions were the International Finance database and the OECD databases, which were used more by departments not engaged in foreign exchange or international lending than by those who were. When grouped by home office and foreign office/branch, the only differences seemed to be for the Foreign Exchange database (Chase Econometrics), which was rated higher by branch offices, and the OECD databases, which were rated higher by home offices.

Using the same clustering algorithm as for the estimated frequencies of contact, no large relatively homogeneous clusters were formed. The BAB and BAI databases did cluster together, and that is understandable since both are produced by the same organization—the Bank of America. Also World Tables and World Debt Tables clustered together and both are produced by the World Bank. Five other databases that formed a cluster were simply among the most frequently used of all thirty-one databases—Flow of Funds, U.S. Weekly Banking, FRBSF, Foreign Exchange, and Merrill Lynch Economics.

Only 29 percent of all respondents thought that another department in their bank might make greater use of such databases. Some 51 percent thought not, and the remainder either did not know or declined to say. Among the departments suggested as ones that might make greater use of the databases were: economic research (16); investments (2); financial analysis; securities research; foreign exchange (4); trading department; arbitrage; syndication; new issues; international treasury (5); trust; money market; and international.

In a few cases, the number of banks reporting use of certain databases can be matched against statistics supplied by database producers in correspondence conducted at about the same time. The Chartered Banks database, for example, is used by seven Canadian banks according to the producer, FRI Information Services Ltd. Five of these banks were represented in the survey, and only two reported using the database. (Four other non-Canadian respondents also reported using the database.) As another example, Compustat Bankfile was reportedly used by twelve banks in the survey but the producer, Standard & Poor, says that the majority of the money-center banks in the United States are users. One of the difficulties in trying to gather figures on database use is the fact that the producer may have no idea who eventually uses the database. The International Monetary Fund produces at least four computerized files that are sold as computer tapes to both individual organizations and to computer network operators. The IMF says that they have about thirty-five banks as direct customers for the tapes and that these banks are generally central banks. However, data from the IMF tapes become part of the Currency Exchange database on the General Electric Mark III network and part of the International Financial Statistics database on the Rapidata network, to name just a few. In fact, the IMF sells tapes to fourteen different subscribers, who resell the data through timesharing services.

The reciprocity measures, in sum, show asymmetrical relationships among the banks regarding telecommunications contact and relatively little joint use of common databases. The rather small number of respondents reporting that their departments used any of the databases may have resulted from the paucity of responses from economic research departments. It seems that the survey results may understate actual use, although it should also be noted that, of all respondents, less than a third believed that any other department in their bank would use any of the databases more than they did.

The standardization measures in the survey found substantial support among respondents. Overwhelmingly, the respondents agreed that their own banks are increasingly using standardized formats or procedures for message traffic among banks and that computer/telecommunications networks encourage the increasing standardization. (See table 4-11.) Some 72 percent of the respondents said that their own organizations are increasingly standardizing

Table 4-11
Attitudes of Respondents Regarding Standardization (N=123)

	Yes	No	Don't Know
Our bank is increasingly using formats or procedures that have been standardized for message traffic among banks.	89	16	18

	Agree			Uncertain		Disagree
Computer/telecommunication networks encourage increasing standardization among international banks.	56	48	2	15	1	1 0

interbank message traffic, and 86 percent agreed with the standardizing role of the computer/telecommunications networks.

Several respondents added that they intend to use SWIFT but are not yet doing so, and one mentioned that some U.K. banks are investigating the possibility of a standard telex format.

One set of questions in the survey concerned the standardization of exchanges in terms of languages. Since written or spoken languages play a major role in information exchange, whether via the telephone or a computer network, the use of one language instead of another might be considered a form of standardization of the unit of exchange. The survey participants were asked to estimate the extent to which their departments used various languages, relative to other languages, for contacting other banks internationally. Specifically, the contacts were limited to telecommunications contacts, that is, by telephone, telex, facsimile, and computer network.

Among respondents whose departments use computer networks and facsimile, along with telephone and telex to contact other banks internationally, English was reportedly used to a greater extent when the mode was a computer communication than when it was telex, telephone, or facsimile, in that order. Respondents estimated that 93 percent of their departments' international computer traffic with other banks was in English, while approximately 87 percent of telex messages, 80 percent of telephone conversations and 76 percent of facsimile traffic were in English. (See table 4-12.) Not all the respondents' departments use all four modes of telecommunications mentioned, of course; although 100 percent of those who answered this section (N=120) said that their departments used the telephone to contact other banks, and 98 percent said that their departments use telex for the same purpose, only 82 percent reported that their departments use computer networks, and only 62 percent said that their departments use facsimile to contact other banks.

Table 4-12
Use of Languages in Telecommunications among Banks
(*percent*)

| | Telecommunications Facility | | | | | | | |
| | Computer Networks (N=98) | | Telex (N=117) | | Telephone (N=120) | | Facsimile (N=74) | |
	mean	*max*	*mean*	*max*	*mean*	*max*	*mean*	*max*
English	92.7	100	86.9	100	79.6	100	76.2	100
French	1.4	50	3.2	40	4.7	50	1.7	50
German	4.1	90	3.3	50	7.0	98	4.4	80
Italian	0.2	5	0.8	30	1.3	40	0.1	10
Japanese	1.6	100	3.2	80	4.0	90	15.2	100
Other	0.2	15	2.6	95	3.5	95	1.1	50

Note: Because not all respondents use the facilities indicated, there are different sizes of *N*. Among all respondents answering this section (120), 100 percent indicated use of the telephone to contact other banks, 98 percent indicated use of telex, 82 percent indicated use of computer networks, and 62 percent indicated use of facsimile.

Again, the estimates ranged widely. For English, the estimates ranged from minimal use to 100 percent for all four of the forms of telecommunications. For French and Italian, the estimates ranged up to about 50 percent usage, as opposed to use of any other language for interbank contacts, by some respondents. For German and Japanese, the estimates ranged up to 100 percent usage for certain forms of telecommunications. For example, some respondents reported that 80 to 90 percent of their telephone conversations with other international banks were in German. Estimates for usage of Japanese ranged up to 100 percent for facsimile and computer communications and nearly as high for telephone and telex. Several Japanese respondents made the comment that all their facsimile traffic was with their head office, and almost all the time it is in Japanese. Looking at the means for each form of telecommunication broken down by language, French, German, and Italian, when used, were used more in telephone conversations than in other modes. Japanese, though, when used, was reportedly used more in facsimile communications.

Since all except a few of the foreign branches or offices were located in New York or London, a greater use of English in telecommunications with other banks might be expected from the branch offices as a whole. Generally this was the case except for facsimile. (See table 4-13.) Foreign branches using facsimile reported 23.4 use of Japanese, and home offices using facsimile reported only 5.3 percent use of Japanese. This is also evident in the breakdowns by country of the home office (table 4-14). Banks with home offices in

Table 4-13
Use of Languages by Respondents at Home Offices and at Foreign Branches or Offices
(percent)

	Telecommunications Facility							
	Computer Networks		Telex		Telephone Conversations		Facsimile	
	Home (N=48)	*Foreign (N=50)*	*Home (N=61)*	*Foreign (N=56)*	*Home (N=64)*	*Foreign (N=56)*	*Home (N=38)*	*Foreign (N=36)*
English	90.1	95.2	86.8	87.0	76.8	82.9	81.4	70.7
French	2.2	0.6	4.2	2.1	6.2	3.0	3.1	0.3
German	5.0	3.1	4.2	2.4	8.6	5.0	4.1	4.6
Italian	0.2	0.1	0.4	1.2	0.6	2.0	0.02	0.3
Japanese	2.2	0.8	1.4	4.0	2.0	4.8	5.3	23.4
Other	0.3	0.1	1.9	3.3	4.6	2.3	1.4	0.7

Table 4-14
Use of Languages in Interbank Telecommunications, by Geographic Area of Home Office
(percent)

Telecommunications Facility

	Computer Networks			Telex			Telephone Conversations			Facsimile		
	Japan (N=21)	North America (N=30)	Western Europe (N=47)	Japan (N=26)	North America (N=33)	Western Europe (N=58)	Japan (N=27)	North America (N=33)	Western Europe (N=60)	Japan (N=18)	North America (N=29)	Western Europe (N=28)
English	92.8	99.9	88.0	86.9	98.4	81.2	82.6	94.0	70.5	32.0	98.9	82.6
French	0	0.03	2.9	0.04	0.5	6.2	0.5	2.1	8.1	0	0.8	3.6
German	0	0	8.4	0	0.4	6.5	0.2	0.9	13.3	0	0.03	11.1
Italian	0	0	0.3	0	0.2	1.5	0.03	0.2	2.3	0	0	0.4
Japanese	7.2	0	0.02	14.5	0.03	0.02	16.3	0.6	0.3	62.4	0.04	0.03
Other	0	0.03	0.4	0.2	0.7	4.7	0.4	2.2	5.7	0	0.3	2.4

Japan reported that 62 percent of their facsimile traffic with other banks was in Japanese.

Another observation from table 4-14 is that banks based in Japan seem to use English in their telecommunications contacts with other banks to a greater degree than do banks based in Western Europe (except, as noted, for facsimile).

Besides the languages listed in the questionnaire (English, French, German, Italian, Japanese), Spanish was mentioned by fourteen respondents for up to 20 percent use in telephone and telex communications. Portuguese was mentioned by four respondents, including one who stated that 95 percent of their telex traffic with other banks was in Portuguese. Other languages noted for their use in interbank telecommunications were Flemish, Dutch, Swedish, and Norwegian.

When asked if other departments might use the various languages to a greater degree, 47 percent of all respondents said yes and 46 percent said no. Some of the other departments mentioned were: various regional offices and foreign branches (9); European lending; international banking (3); international department or division (8); foreign exchange (8); international finance (2); foreign department (2); syndication (2); overseas division (2); letters of credit (3); international funds; international business operations; money transfer; bullion; shares trading; bond placement; interbank traders; leasing; securities (3); trade; communications; financial; commercial (3); customer relations; correspondent banking; and world corporate.

There seems to be no doubt, then, that interbank message traffic is becoming more standardized, at least in the minds of personnel at the largest commercial banks. And, although no cause-and-effect relationship can be established, it seems as if computer networks are playing a role in that standardization, even to the extent of encouraging wider use of the English language in interbank communications. (Naturally, as the estimates indicate, English is already used widely, although not universally, and there are many cultural, political, and social reasons why this is so.)

Finally, in an attempt to place the information exchange among banks into perspective, participants were asked to divide their "total information exchange activities" into activity within the department, activity within the organization but crossing departmental lines, activity among banks in general, activity with clients or customers, and "other."

Respondents estimated that about 28 percent of their departments' total "information exchange activities" occurred within the department, with 25 percent of such activity occurring within the organization among departments. The two other major areas of information exchange activity—with other banks, and with clients or customers—received mean estimates of 22 percent and 20 percent respectively. (See table 4-15.)

Dividing the responses by geographic area (on the basis of the country of the home office) revealed some minor differences. The Western European

Table 4-15
Breakdown of Total Information Exchange Activity (N=112)
(percent)

					Average Day								Mean	Standard Deviation
	0	1-10	20	30	40	50	60	70	80	90	100			
Within department	12	11	27	26	9	19	4	2	2	–	–		28.42	18.5
Within the bank	4	20	35	32	9	7	1	1	1	1	1		25.30	16.8
With other banks	7	36	27	16	14	10	–	–	1	1	–		21.91	17.0
With clients	6	33	33	22	11	6	–	–	1	–	–		20.43	14.1
Other	63	41	5	2	1	–	–	–	–	–	–		4.39	6.8

Note: Cell counts are the numbers of respondents giving estimates in the ranges indicated.

group gave higher estimates for activity among banks and lower estimates for activity within the department than did the North American or Japanese groups (see group means, table 4-16).

The breakdown by major activity was somewhat clouded by the high number of respondents who checked both foreign exchange and international lending as their major activities. However, respondents who did not check either of these categories reported the highest estimate for information exchange within the organization (29 percent of all such activity) and the lowest estimate for activity among banks (19 percent of information exchange activity).

There were no real differences in the estimates when respondents from home offices were grouped apart from respondents from foreign branches or offices.

Again, a few people indicated that they could not give estimates. One wrote "impossible to assess!" and another wrote that estimates for his division

Table 4-16
Average Information Exchange Activity, by Subgroup (N=112)
(*percent*)

	Japan	*North America*	*Western Europe*	*Group Means*
Within department				
Home	32.9	29.5	25.1	28.2
Branch	32.5	31.9	24.1	28.7
Group means	32.7	30.4	24.7	
Among departments				
Home	23.8	27.9	24.4	25.5
Branch	27.8	20.4	25.9	25.1
Group means	26.1	25.0	25.1	
Among banks				
Home	20.5	17.7	25.8	22.0
Branch	15.6	19.8	27.6	21.9
Group means	17.7	18.5	26.6	
With customers				
Home	18.3	20.5	19.8	19.7
Branch	20.3	25.0	19.8	21.3
Group means	19.4	22.2	19.8	
Other				
Home	3.1	6.3	6.4	5.7
Branch	3.8	1.4	3.0	2.8
Group means	3.5	4.4	4.9	

would be inappropriate. Relatively few respondents alloted any portion of the information exchange activity to the "other" category; one who did so specified that it was largely public relations and related matters.

The respondents in the survey, then, estimated that twice as much information exchange took place within the organization as among banks but that information exchange with other banks rivaled that with clients or customers.

The net indication of the survey's measures of interorganization relations is one of high formalization, high but uneven intensity (frequency of contact), reliance on the telephone and telex more than on computer networks, low (or unknown) sharing of the same economic databases, and high standardization either in effect now or expected as a matter of course. As a group, the Western European-based banks exhibited a higher degree of interorganization information exchange via telecommunications and computers than did either the Japanese or North American banks. In the following chapter, these indications will be matched with other indications of the telecommunications relationships among the largest commercial banks as these relationships have developed in recent history.

Notes

1. Cora Bagley Marrett, "On the Specification of Interorganizational Dimensions," *Sociology and Social Research* 56 (October 1971): 83-99.

2. Howard Aldrich, *Organizations and Environments* (Englewood Cliffs, N.J.: Prentice-Hall, 1979). See also Benson, Evan, Pfeffer and Salancik, Stern, Tuite et al., Turk, and Whetten and Leung for their respective works on interorganization relations, listed in the bibliography.

3. Herbert A. Simon, *The New Science of Management Decision* (Englewood Cliffs, N.J.: Prentice-Hall, 1977), pp. 96-99.

4. The fifty banks were chosen from the following lists: *Moody's Bank and Finance Manual*, 1978 (forty-eight of the top fifty), and 1979 (forty-seven of the top fifty); *Fortune*, 1978 (the eight largest U.S. banks), and 1979 (thirty-nine of the top fifty non-U.S. banks); *World Banking 78-79* (forty-one of the top fifty); and *The Banker*, June 1979 (forty-five of the top fifty).

5. Richard H. Veith, "Information Processing Networks in International Banking," *Social Science Information Studies* 2 (to be published in early 1981).

6. Principle components analysis, varimax rotation, Biomedical Computer Programs, BMD P4M.

7. Clustering algorithm, Biomedical Computer Programs, BMD P1M.

5 Dimensions of Interbank Relations

As human organizations have developed in size and complexity, the interorganization relations have become more complex. The introduction and refinement of techniques and equipment for long-distance, high-volume transmission of messages has been a contributing factor in the global expansion of organizations and subsequent increases in the degree and extent of interorganization contact.

In the following chapter, the four dimensions of interorganization relations—formalization, intensity, reciprocity, and standardization—are used to place the analysis of interorganization relations within a historical and environmental perspective. Such an analysis will suggest some specific contributions of computer/telecommunications to interbank relations. The necessity of the historical viewpoint has been stressed by past researchers and thus is an integral part of the discussion here.

Formalization

Formalization is the degree to which official sanction is given to the interorganization relations, either directly or through an intermediary such as a government. As will be seen, banking has become an area of high formalization of interorganization relations.

In the United States, the earliest banks operated more or less as completely independent businesses until the proliferation of banks and the need for reliable commercial banknotes in the 1800s resulted in both legislative and nonlegislative efforts to formalize interbank exchanges.[1] For example, in the nonlegislative area, clearing houses were established to allow banks in a given geographic area to settle accounts with each other promptly and efficiently. The New York Clearing House was established in 1853, the Boston Clearing House in 1856, and the Philadelphia Clearing House in 1858. On the legislative side, one of the requirements of the National Bank Act of 1863 was that national banknotes be similar in design and be accepted at all national banks at par value. The desire to smooth out periodic fluctuations in the demands for currency and bank reserves led to the establishment of the Federal Reserve System in 1913, which in effect pooled the reserves of member banks and also allowed member banks to increase their reserves.

The foreign activities of U.S. banks came under the provisions of the

Federal Reserve Act with the Edge Act Amendment of 1919. The regulations affecting foreign banking have since then been periodically revised by the Federal Reserve Board and by specific legislation. In addition, foreign branches of banks are subject to host country laws and such international treaties as Great Britain's Convention of Commerce and Navigation of 1815, Switzerland's Convention of Friendship, Commerce and Extradition of 1850, and France's Convention of Establishment of 1959. State regulations are sometimes also pertinent. The New York State Banking Department, for example, examines the financial operation of overseas branches of New York banks.

One of the primary examples of agreement formalization, that is, officially sanctioned relationships, is the arrangement known as correspondent banking, where banks leave money on account at other banks in the large money centers in return for services. On the international level, a correspondent bank is a domestic bank that acts as the agent for a foreign bank for the purpose of processing transactions. Correspondent activities might involve accepting drafts, honoring letters of credit, or furnishing credit information.

International banking grew and prospered because of the traditional network of correspondent banking organizations.[2] And the international link between correspondent banks of different countries has been maintained primarily through the use of telecommunications and the mails.[3] Even when a bank decides to open its own representative office, or even a branch, in a foreign country, the existing correspondent relationships are often continued. The major commercial banks have correspondent relationships with banks in most of the principal cities of the world. Manufacturers Hanover Trust Company, for example, has correspondent relations with twenty-seven hundred banks in the United States and seventeen hundred banks outside the country.

A second area of strong agreement formalization is that of the Eurocurrency market and the syndicated loan. (Eurocurrencies are bank deposits held outside the country of issue. These are primarily U.S. dollars and European currencies held in Europe.) The Eurocurrency market began to be recognized as such during the mid 1950s and began to grow rapidly as a result of, among other things, the British balance of payments crisis in 1959, tight money in the United States in 1959, and the overseas expansion of U.S. banks in the 1960s. The Eurocurrency market is now said to have overshadowed national markets and to be composed of apparently stateless money.[4] In other words, much of the money in the market cannot be regulated or governed by any single country.

Telecommunications have played an important role in the establishment of a large Eurocurrency market. According to a book by Stuart Robinson, the teleprinter and the telephone permitted foreign exchange dealers to readily trade Eurocurrencies, building on preexisting relationships.[5] Another account tells of million-dollar lots traded wholesale over telephone and telex and of banks calling all over Europe to seek Eurodollar deposits.[6] The chairman of

Citicorp has noted that technology did not create the Euromarkets (regulations did that), but it did nourish the markets such that transactions are processed increasingly faster and more efficiently.[7] Although the Eurocurrency market used to be dominated by about twenty banks, the major activity is now spread out among about two hundred banks.[8]

The rapid information exchange via telecommunications has been of particular importance in arranging syndicated Eurocurrency loans. One banking official rates the syndicated loan as the world's premier financing vehicle and attributes the Eurocurrency syndicated loan to the availability of telecommunications facilities as well as to larger reasons such as the need of governments and multinationals for ample sources of funds, the increasing size of loans, the desire to spread the risks, and the desire to form working relationships with other banks.[9] In most cases, when a bank acting as the syndicate leader is ready to "sell" the loan to other banks, the general terms and conditions are sent out by telex or discussed by telephone. Interested banks then receive more complete written documentation. The loan arrangements may be offered to as many as two hundred fifty banks, and an actual Euromarket loan might have over a hundred participating banks.

Historically, U.S. banks have found that to enter the Euromarket it not only was necessary to establish branches in Europe but also was quite useful to form banking consortia; the consortia in fact were almost forced on the banks by the competition to diversify.[10] The U.S. banks needed to increase the range of their services to match the customary activities of other international banks, and a primary means of doing so was to engage in joint undertakings with foreign banks.

The second type of formalization—structural formalization—the coordinating effect of an intermediary, is rather obvious in banking. The most prominent example is government regulation. In the United States, structural formalization occurs not only through the Federal Reserve System and federal banking laws but also through state banking regulations, the regulations of the Federal Deposit Insurance Corporation (FDIC), and for national banks the regulations of the comptroller of the currency within the Treasury Department.

Banking regulations and economic controls do not necessarily always have a coordinating effect on interbank relations, but indirectly economic controls have certainly encouraged increased multinational banking by U.S. banks. The introduction of controls in the 1960s provided the primary impetus behind the overseas expansion of that decade.[11]

Generally, there is also strong structural formalization in the form of central banking systems. Central banks directly or indirectly affect the relationships among banks. The Deutsche Bundesbank is responsible for playing a general role in the supervison of West German banks as well as setting monetary and credit policy. The Bank of England has direct authority over banks but has preferred usually to act informally to promote orderly financial markets. The Banque de France, along with normal central banking functions, is the decision maker in regulating the banking profession and banking practices. In the Netherlands, the Nederlandsche Bank can issue general instructions directly to banks with the consent of the minister of finance.[12]

During the years since World War II, the central banks of the industrialized countries have often found occasion to either work together or to adopt similar strategies to manage world traffic in currencies. During the 1950s, central banks and governments of Western Europe held as a major policy goal the maintenance of economic growth and security and the convertibility of currencies. In 1962, the Federal Reserve System in the United States entered into a number of arrangements, for example, with foreign central banks to moderate exchange-rate fluctuations. Cooperative measures by central banks began to be strengthened in the 1960s and expanded during the late 1960s and into the 1970s. In 1974, for example, the mere report that three central banks had reached an agreement on concerted action halted a slide in the dollar's relative value.[13]

The cooperation among central banks seems not only to have continually increased but also to have expanded to include regulatory policies, largely because of the speed and volume of worldwide information exchanges. In 1975, the Federal Reserve noted that monetary policies were becoming internationally interrelated because of faster transmission and processing of economic data and because of improved technology for handling payments.[14] In 1977, the cooperation among central banks was also credited with providing more information to commercial banks regarding external borrowings and external indebtedness.[15]

In a related form of structural formalization, the Western countries have been discussing international monetary reform, and France is to submit new proposals for structuring the international system.[16]

Concentrating on structural formalization in computer/telecommunications, a number of intermediaries have established or have adopted the use of automated-network facilities. For instance, Bank Wire is an organization cooperatively owned by several hundred banks established for the purpose of transfering funds messages electronically among banks. Fed Wire and the Clearing House Interbank Payments System (CHIPS) are both computerized networks that grew out of existing exchange relationships among the banks. In the United States, large money transfers via wire have been regularly accomplished since the mid-1930s and were automated in the 1970s. Internationally, the Society for Worldwide Interbank Financial Telecommunication (SWIFT) was established in 1973 by 240 Western European and North American banks to improve the contacts among correspondent banks. (It might be noted that central banks as well as commercial banks are members of SWIFT, and the Federal Reserve was one of the original sponsors of the SWIFT feasibility studies.) SWIFT is organized as a nonprofit cooperative society under Belgian law and is wholly owned by member banks, with shares distributed according to the volume of message traffic.

The development of SWIFT required not only technical agreements binding on member banks but also procedural agreements, that is, the formalization of certain banking practices. The latter task required considerable liaison among the banks of different countries and involved the establishment of a Standards Committee with representatives nominated from each member country. Since the network has been in operation, all member countries continue to have national user groups, and each country elects one person to serve on the board. The board is responsible for reviewing and setting policy as well as handling applications for membership. SWIFT, therefore, is an intermediary organization that has caused some uniformity in international banking procedures for exchanges, governed by elected representatives for different banks on a country-by-country basis.

The CHIPS network is also an international facility in that foreign banks are members. (It is reported that 90 percent of the dollars that move internationally in the noncommunist world move through CHIPS at some point.) However the network has a two-tier membership structure giving the New York Clearing House banks control over operations and over access by foreign banks. (This structure is now in the process of being modified.) One of the results of the use of the network has been a slight shortening of the deadline for clearing. Since 1863, clearing through the New York Clearing House had been accomplished by the following day; in recent times the deadline was 1 P.M. In July 1979, amid a certain amount of controversy, the deadline was advanced three hours to 10 A.M.[17] The purpose of the advance was to begin a series of steps that will eventually result in same-day settlement.

More importantly, the efficiency of the CHIPS network as a computerized information transfer system has contributed to the rapidly expanding volume of international payment transactions.[18]

Along the same lines, a study of electronic funds transfer (EFT) has concluded that eventually EFT facilities will provide for increased international currency transactions, increased convenience and security, increased interdependence of monetary policies, and some coordination of supervisory policies over multinational banks.[19] At the time of the study (1977), Europe was said to be more advanced than the United States in use of automatic clearing centers. The study also reported that in Europe and Japan banks share technology and networks and cooperate with each other to compete with other deposit-taking institutions.

In comparing these indications of formalization with the survey results given in the preceding chapter, it is clear that a high degree of formalization exists in banking generally, and it has existed for some time. This formalization, though, exists to a lesser extent in international banking; for example, there is no multinational or supranational governing body. A massive activity such as the Euromarket is relatively free of a regulatory agency. Yet agreement formalization, that is, official relationships among the banks themselves, is quite high. The internationally syndicated loan market is vast in monetary terms and involves most of if not all the major international banks in joint projects. (Among survey participants, 85 percent said that their own banks were increasingly involved in syndicated loans.) In another sense there is a high degree of agreement formalization in the activities of the major central banks as a group, who often engage in joint efforts to maintain orderly markets and stable economies.

Historically, there is ample support for high degrees of both agreement formalization and structural formalization. And, since the 1950s, both types of formalization have been affected by the availability of telecommunications and computers, as well as by other general changes. By the end of that decade, for example, regular trans-Atlantic jet service was permitting banks and other multinational organizations to keep in close physical contact, the telephone networks in international banking were becoming vital to daily operations, economic and political stability in Western Europe was increasing, the European Monetary Act had been signed in 1955, and various steps were being taken to improve international and regional cooperation.[20]

Intensity

Intensity refers to the size of the resource investment in interorganization relations and the frequency of interaction. One measure of the size of resource investment is the amount of commitment to syndicated loans, which rely heavily on telecommunications for effective coordination. In 1975 the average syndicated loan was $50 million, with some loans exceeding $1 billion. The total volume of the Euromarket, including loans and bond issues, is somewhat difficult to estimate, but one 1979 estimate was $95 billion and another estimate went as high as $1 trillion.[21] By any count, the total monetary obligations among banks of various countries is a massive amount.[22]

One of the elements of the syndicated loan, by definition, is that it is spread out among a number of banks, often from different countries. For example, a Eurodollar loan in 1979 to an enterprise owned jointly by Argentina and Paraguay had six lead managers (banks from Japan, the United States, Canada, and Switzerland), six managers (banks from Argentina, Italy, Germany, France, and Great Britain), and seventeen comanagers. (Banks acting as lead managers, managers, and comanagers have varying degrees of responsibility in arranging the loan and in monitoring the project.) The total amount of the loan, $200 million, was provided by thirty-seven banks from sixteen countries. On the other hand, a 10.8 billion yen loan to Australia's Qantas Airlines at about the same time had four Japanese banks as managers and comanagers, and the funds were provided by only eleven Japanese banks altogether.

Interestingly, the growth of international banking and multinational Eurodollar loans in the 1960s and 1970s was not a result of a desire for increased cooperation among banks but rather was the result of competition. In the United States, for example, major banks began entering the international market largely because they felt that they would lose business if they did not.[23] The competition was spurred by the desire not only to win profits and maintain a competitive position but also to have access to sources of foreign funding when or if domestic monetary policies tightened sources at home. Increased interbank relationships in the form of consortia, joint ventures, and syndicates were the vehicles for such expansion.

Another measure of resource investment appropriate for international relations via telecommunications is the investment in SWIFT, although SWIFT is certainly not the sole facility for international exchanges accomplished electronically. To become a SWIFT member, each bank pays a one-time fee, which is determined annually and is designed to recover the costs for interface connection equipment in general. In addition there are direct recurring costs based on actual volume of use and on costs for general software maintenance. During 1978 the unit charge for normal messages was 14 Belgian francs (about 50 cents), twice that for urgent messages, or half that for low-priority messages. Assuming an average daily volume of 160,000 messages, and using the normal charge for each message, the member banks of SWIFT are collectively paying some $80,000 a day to transmit messages to other banks.

A third measure of intensity is the overall investment in telecommunications service. In the United States, a number of surveys undertaken periodically have sought to discover how much is spent by U.S. banks for telecommunications.[24] Approximately $640 million was spent on telecommunications in 1975, and an estimated $788 million was spent in 1978 (by all U.S. banks). Approximately 80 percent of this money goes for simple telephone service. In 1975, less than 40 percent of the total was for long-distance telecommunication, and only 40 percent of that was attributed to interbank communication. Assuming that the great majority of interbank communication is indeed conducted via telecommunications, this agrees roughly with the estimations reported in the preceding chapter, that is, that about 20 percent of all information exchange takes place with other banks. Regarding investment in telecommunications as a percentage of all expenses, though, money spent for telecommunications is said to be only slightly over 2 percent of total nonfinancial operating expenses for the larger banks.

Resource investment appears to be high, then, on the basis of estimates of the size of the syndicated loan market, the investments in SWIFT and similar networks, and the investments in maintaining cordial correspondent relations, but the actual cost of telecommunications and data networks is a minor part of operating budgets.

The second type of intensity, frequency of interaction, also would appear to be quite high. Telecommunications contact among correspondent banks and trading partners is almost continuous during most of the working day. Several of the respondents in the survey of the previous chapter emphasized the extreme frequency of telecommunications contact among certain departments of major banks, such as the foreign exchange dealers.

Overall, the survey's participants estimated that their departments spend, on the average, a third of the day in telecommunications contact with other banks. This may or may not be high frequency, but in response to another question, the amount of information exchange of any kind with other banks was the largest of such categories of activities outside of information exchange within the organization. Another finding of the survey was that frequency of contact is not uniform geographically. Using the estimated frequency of contact with other banks, the Western European banks clustered together as did the U.S. banks and, in a third group, the Japanese banks. Modern telecommunications have not yet obliterated the effects of geographic location.

The frequency of contact is of course not solely dependent on telecommunications channels being available. The efficiency of the early Eurodollar market has been related to the physical presence of banks and bankers in London and to their long-established techniques for doing business with each other. Robinson presents the web of banks situated near the Bank of England as the basis for an efficient Eurodollar marketplace in the 1960s and 1970s.[25] As noted in the previous chapter, bankers in London rely on messenger service as well as on the post and the telephone for exchanges within the city.

In sum, there is little doubt that banking, at least during this century, exhibits a rather high intensity of interorganization relations. There is also evidence that, although the intensity of interbank relations was already high, and high regarding telecommunications specifically, some incremental change is taking place in the realm of computer networks. Banks have invested in joint networks and are investing in the use of information files produced by other banks and distributed via computer networks. At this time, computer network use is relatively minor in comparison to other forms of telecommunications-related and non-telecommunications contacts and exchanges among banks. Within the next ten or fifteen years this may change, but it is difficult and perhaps impossible to state that the overall intensity of interorganization relations will be substantially increased as a result.

Reciprocity

Reciprocity refers to the balance or symmetry of the interorganization relations, and in interorganization studies this often refers to the balance of power. The balance of power among the major commercial banks is neither even nor necessarily stable. In simple terms, the rank order of the largest banks has changed over time. In the ten years ending in 1979, for example, two British banks dropped from the first and second place on the 1969 list of the largest non-U.S. banks to fifteenth and nineteenth places respectively, and the third place bank in 1969, an Italian bank, dropped to thirtieth place.[26]

In the Euromarket, world events and various domestic monetary policies also affect the participation of given banks. The Europmarket was once dominated by U.S. banks, but in 1979 the market was the province of Japanese, Swiss, and West German banks.[27]

One of the types of reciprocity, the extent to which the conditions of exchange are agreed on mutually, is apparently occurring among international banks of the industrialized countries on a balanced scale. There is evidence that there has been a two-way flow, that is, between home and host countries, of banking techniques and an appreciation of another country's banking procedures and customs.[28]

Looking at the specific contribution of computer/telecommunications to reciprocal flow of resources, internal telecommunications networks at least have given some banks a competitive edge. With regard to the networks and the Eurodollar market, Robinson asserts that use of the networks reduces delay, puts participants in faster and more direct contact, permits less expensive transfer of deposits, and allows the banks to be free of the constraints of any local market.[29] Thus banks with internal networks began to have an advantage over banks that did not have internal networks.

In the future, computer/telecommunications networks may give a similar sort of edge to groups of banks using interconnected networks. As mentioned in chapter 3, several major banks, for example, are developing electronic mail systems for loan syndication activites. It is not inconceivable that these will be interconnected for documentary exchanges.

Another effect of the internal telecommunications networks that might be considered under the heading of reciprocity is the growing independence of overseas branches. During the 1960s and 1970s, the U.S. branch banks in foreign countries exhibited a considerable amount of independence in their relationships with their home offices.[30] This apparently resulted from the nature of U.S. economic policy at the time, the nature of the Eurocurrency market, and various host country laws, but the underlying facilitating agent was the availability of rapid communications among an organization's network of branches. Thus, the telecommunications and computer networks permitted organizations to expand and at the same time experience more independence of distant units—which could still remain an integral part of the whole.

In the survey's results in chapter 4, no direct measure of resource reciprocity was attempted, although an analysis of frequency of telecommunications contact showed that some banks were the recipients of more telecommunications than were other banks. This might indicate the direction of flows of resources, since one of the major purposes of interbank telecommunications is the transfer of funds or of information relating to the transfer of funds. The banks receiving the most frequent amount of telecommunications contact were the U.S. banks followed by the U.K. banks.

An attempt within the survey to gauge the flow of economic data through the use of specific databases produced little evidence of either even or uneven flows of information. This may have resulted from the low number of responses from economic research departments or from a real condition of relatively low levels of use. The most that can be said is that the more used databases of those listed in the questionnaire were databases compiled by banks and by central banks.

Historical evidence, in short, does indicate that advanced computer/tele-communications networks do have an effect on the competitive advantage of given organizations. This in turn contributes to other factors, which affect the power balance among the organizations in a group or industry. Internationally, SWIFT may begin to exert some influence over the flow of resources by virtue of offering more secure and more efficient means of sending interbank messages and by promulgating procedures for settling differences among members over liability in cases of error or malfunction. If internal computer/tele-communications networks were beneficial because they allowed the organization to function more efficiently in a more coordinated manner, then interorganizational networks may enable groups of banks from different countries to engage in more cooperative efforts.

Standardization

Standardization of the unit of exchange and procedures for exchange is very evident in banking in several areas. First of all, there have been continuing efforts to establish standards for monetary exchanges. The International Monetary Fund and the World Bank, the Bank for International Settlements, the General Agreements on Tariffs and Trade (GATT), the European Common Market agreements, and the creation of the European Monetary System all are areas where concerted effort has taken place to promote stability and to establish international cooperation. As an example of such agreements leading to standardization, the European Community has been attempting to harmonize corporate law, hoping to produce Communitywide agreements on antitrust violations and eventually the standardization of accounting and reporting procedures for corporations. And the European Monetary System, in effect since March 1979, links the currencies in the European Community to fixed exchange rates with the eventual goal of monetary unification and a single currency.

In the area of telecommunications, standardization has proceeded on several fronts, often encompassing both technical and procedural standards. In the United States, the Bank Administration Institute (a nonprofit corporation engaged in banking research and education) has published a number of communications standards for banks as the only practical way of producing efficient electronic-information systems among banks.[31] Internationally, SWIFT has standarized message formats for certain types of interbank exchanges. According to some in the banking industry, no progress at all had been made in achieving such standardization until the SWIFT network was created.

As mentioned in chapter 4, the participants in the survey of the largest banks agreed that they are increasingly using standardized formats for interbank messages and that computer/telecommunications networks encourage that standardization. It also appeared that computer networks are playing a standardizing role in being associated with more use of the English language for interbank communication than other forms of telecommunications.

A more encompassing series of steps toward telecommunications standardization has been in the general area of transborder data flow. The conventions or treaties, conferences, and legislation discussed in chapter 2 are perhaps the most influential attempts internationally to arrive at some cooperative, harmonized procedures for all manner of data traffic. This is seen as desirable because of the need to provide protection for each country's own citizens and to extend protection of data to another country's physical space. These measures have stemmed from very powerful arguments regarding personal privacy, economic balance, and national sovereignty and are seen as central to the healthy life of nations in the future.

Taken together, the dimensions of formalization, intensity, reciprocity, and standardization have provided a means of isolating the specific contributions of computer/telecommunications to interorganization relations. In the concluding chapter, these will be summarized and related to the larger question of the social impact of transborder networks for information processing.

Notes

1. Richard H. Timberlake, Jr., *Money, Banking and Central Banking* (New York: Harper and Row, 1965).

2. Martin Mayer, *The Bankers* (New York: Weybright and Talley, 1974), p. 432.

3. Stuart W. Robinson, Jr., *Multinational Banking* (Leiden: A.W. Sijthoff, 1972), pp. 20-21.

4. P. Henry Mueller, "A Conspectus for Offshore Lenders," in *Offshore Lending by U.S. Commercial Banks,* ed. F. John Mathis (Washington, D.C.: Bankers' Association for Foreign Trade, 1975), pp. 23-24.

5. Robinson, *Multinational Banking*, p. 195.

6. From a report in *Barron's* quoted in P. Henry Muller, "A Conspectus for Offshore Lenders," in *Offshore Lending,* ed. Mathis, p. 24.

7. Walter B. Wriston, "The Euromarkets: Offspring of Technology," *American Banker,* 28 September 1979, pp. 16, 58.

8. Edward Meadows, "How the Euromarket Fends Off Global Financial Disaster," *Fortune,* 24 September 1979, pp. 122-135.

9. Robert N. Bee, "Syndication," in *Offshore Lending*, ed. Mathis, pp. 151-152.

10. James C. Baker and M. Gerald Bradford, *American Banks Abroad* (New York: Praeger, 1974), pp. 12-13.

11. P. Henry Mueller, "A Conspectus for Offshore Lenders," in *Offshore Lending*, ed. Mathis, p. 4.

12. See, for example, Bank for International Settlements, *Eight European Central Banks* (New York: Frederick A. Praeger, 1965).

13. *Annual Report of the Board of Governors of the Federal Reserve System* (Washington, D.C., 1974), p. 65.

14. *Annual Report of the Board of Governors of the Federal Reserve System* (Washington, D.C., 1975), p. 262.

15. *Annual Report of the Board of Governors of the Federal Reserve System* (Washington, D.C., 1977), p. 419.

16. Paul Lewis, "A New Monetarism Sweeps the West," International Economic Survey Section, *New York Times,* 3 February 1980, p. 14.

17. Wayne B. Lewin and David Van L. Taylor, "CHIPS, an Evolving Electronic Funds Transfer System," *Bank Administration* 55 (November 1979): 36-39.

18. Ibid.

19. National Commission on Electronic Fund Transfers, *EFT in the United States* (Washington, D.C.: U.S. Government Printing Office, 1977), pp. 222-234.

20. Robinson, *Multinational Banking*, p. 155.

21. Ann Crittenden, "A Boom in 'No-Strings' Banking," *New York Times,* 3 February 1980, sect. 12, p. 26.

22. Charles S. Ganoe, "Loans and Placements to Foreign Banks," in *Offshore Lending* ed. Mathis, p. 167.

23. Charles M. Williams, "International Lending in the Decade Ahead: An Overview," in *Offshore Lending*, ed. Mathis, p. 234.

24. See, for example, "Bank Talk Is Far from Cheap," *Bank Systems and Equipment* 15 (April 1978): 61-62; "ABA Surveying Bank Voice, Data Transmissions," *American Banker*, 20 February 1979, p. 2; Arnold Kaplan and Per Lange, "Highlights from the '79 Bank Telecommunications Survey," *ABA Banking Journal*, February 1980, pp. 92-95. The most recent survey was aimed at 3,000 banks, and the response rate was 25 percent.

25. Robinson, *Multinational Banking*, p. 196.

26. Hugh M. Hyde, Jr., "The Fortune Directory of the Fifty Largest Commercial Banking Companies outside the U.S.," *Fortune*, 13 August 1979, p. 206.

27. Karen W. Arenson, "Battered Euromarket Thrives," International Economic Survey Section, *New York Times*, 3 February 1980, sect. 12, p. 23.

28. Robinson, *Multinational Banking*, p. 289.

29. Ibid., pp. 195-196.

30. Ibid., p. 291.

31. T.C. Thompson and R.H. Long, *Lock Box Communication Standards for Banks* (Park Ridge, Ill.: Bank Administration Institute, 1972), p. 2.

6 The Organization of Interrelations

The suggestion that technology affects society in important ways is generally accepted. The belief that mankind has the power to control, and to not be controlled by, technology is also widely held. The problem is to understand the intricate, seesaw balance between technology's effects on society and society's creation of technology. One of the more recent technological developments has been the establishment of international computer networks for information processing. These networks link parts of organizations together and link large organizations to each other with channels for high-speed, high-volume transfer of information and large-scale facilities for manipulating and processing the information. The potential of these networks for affecting social organizations is substantial.

This research is an investigation of one industry's use of international computer networks. As Herbert Simon has said, organizational form is a joint function of the people involved, their tools, and the task.[1] If one of these elements changes substantially, the organizational form can be expected to change. In the present case, in international banking, the tools have changed and are changing substantially. In the last ten years or so large-scale computer networks crossing national borders have come into major use. To delve into some of the specifics of the real changes and the anticipated changes, techniques of interorganization relations research were adopted. The techniques were used to understand what the situation was before computers and telecommunications networks, what the situation is now, and what the situation might become.

It might be helpful here to review the particular methodology that was used in this study and why it was selected. Roberts et al., in *Developing an Interdisciplinary Science of Organizations*, emphasize the difficulty and complexity of studying organizational processes.[2] There are a great many ways to attack the problem, and a number of academic disciplines involved; rarely do researchers try to operate simultaneously on the individual, group, organizational, and environmental levels. Instead, researchers use various approaches or models, such as the *sociological paradigm* or model. In this model, the premise is that patterns of social interaction can be observed for an organization as a collective body. Thus, this model does not address individual responses. Instead individuals are taken into account as the elements of the organization that produce the patterns. The choice of a model also implies a certain approach to organizational communication, and in the sociological model communication is assumed to be associated with organizational positions, that is, the communication is not assessed with reference to individuals but may, as in this case, utilize aggregate responses.

In this study of interbank relations, as in the sociological paradigm in general, the unit of analysis is the community, or in this instance the network of interorganization relations. In addition, the importance of understanding historical developments was accepted. Aldrich argues that in the 1960s organizational sociologists failed to contribute to the understanding of organizations by virtue of neglecting to ground their studies in a political and historical context.[3]

One of the procedures for studying interorganization relations while incorporating the ability to weigh political and historical developments is to use some categorization scheme that permits monitoring the relations. The scheme adopted here specifies the four dimensions of formalization, intensity, reciprocity, and standardization. These dimensions were used to assess not only the present state of computer/telecommunications relations in international banking but also the historical development of both interbank relations in general and computer/telecommunications-based relations in particular.

Historically, financial systems in the industrialized countries have exhibited certain common features, despite distinctive legal, social, and political traditions in each country.[4] Since World War II, as economies and political and social systems have become more interdependent, the relationships among banks have similarly become more intertwined. Apart from computer/telecommunications issues, a recent study published in a banking journal concluded that the large commercial banks of the industrialized countries are growing more alike and that their similarities are more important than their different national characteristics or their different organizational structures and practices.[5]

This final chapter summarizes the specific contributions of computer/telecommunications to the interrelationships using the interorganizational dimensions outlined previously. The developments in banking are then related to organizational developments in general and to the larger topic of an information-based society.

Dimensions Summarized

Having been guided by a research method that isolates distinct dimensions of interorganization relations, it is now possible to step back and summarize what the investigation has produced. On the basis of evidence in the literature, correspondence with bankers, and a survey among the largest commercial banks, the following results seem apparent:

Computer/telecommunications in international banking have been related to increased formalization in an industry that historically has been highly formalized.

The interorganizational telecommunications have also provided the means for a high degree of intensity of relations, although the importance of physical closeness cannot be ignored or depreciated.

Information processing networks carrying the same economic databases to banks as a group do exist but at present do not seem to be widely used by the same set of banks.

Internationally, the flow of resources among banks is not uniform, for political and economic reasons that go far beyond computers and tele-communications.

In some specific areas, computerized networks are being expanded to supplement and eventually to replace telex and telephone-based networks.

Standardization is almost a foregone conclusion in computerized telecom-munications and has been a key to the success of SWIFT.

Standardization accompanying the use of computers affects both technical and nontechnical procedures.

Computer networks are associated with greater use of the English language than are other modes of telecommunications contact.

On balance, computerized information processing networks in international banking have allowed the larger banks to facilitate, strengthen, and improve the efficiency of their existing relationships based on telecommunications. If the formalization and standardization continues, the cluster of the largest commer-cial banks may begin to look more and more like a supraorganization, maintain-ing itself and coordinating its activities and objectives with extensive, high-speed, high-volume lines of communication. This does not mean, however, that this cluster organization or supraorganization will act to close its boundaries to newcomers or to support failing members artificially. There is every indication that, as in the past, the actual membership of the cluster organization will fluc-tuate as some banks gain over others in size, assets, scope of operations, and the like. The results indicate that the power balance is neither even nor fixed and that banks leading the group now may not be doing so a decade later.

Yet it also seems that the group of banks involved are, or will be, something more than an industry grouping—more complex, more coordinated, more inter-linked. A senior officer at Citibank has written that the future of what he calls group banking—banks engaged in consortium banking or cooperative activities— depends on the ability to coordinate effectively, on top management dedica-tion to joint enterprises, on the availability of capable people to manage the activity, and on sustained independence of decision making by the senior executives of the participating institutions.[6] Both the first and the last point appear to have been helped by telecommunications networks and computers. Such networks have permitted more coordinated activity while enabling branches to become independent. To restate, the use of the networks seems to be contributing to a collegial form of supraorganization.

Organizational Impact

Although the primary emphasis of this study has been on the relations among organizations, the impact of computer/telecommunications within organizations has not been ignored. In banking specifically, automation has proceeded from computer processing of accounting information and computer-assisted check handling to geographically dispersed computer/telecommunications systems for a variety of banking activities. These systems serve other banks, corporate and group clients, and the public.

At the present time, the use of computerized information processing networks is limited generally to the larger banks. Bank automation surveys have indicated that in 1979 only 15 percent of U.S. banks were online to a computer for automated banking services, and only the large banks were involved in extensive computer/telecommunications. In time, the techniques and facilities employed by the largest organizations will probably be adopted by the medium-size organizations and eventually perhaps by the small organizations.

It has also been a matter of time for the effects of automation suspected in the early 1960s to become visible, although often not in quite the same way as expected. Aldom's 1963 book, *Automation in Banking*, suggested that the Federal Reserve Banks would play a central role in automated money transfer. That has indeed happened, although the Federal Reserve does not operate the only interbank computerized network for either funds transfers or messages regarding debits and credits. In his 1964 *Automation in Commercial Banking*, Yavitz reported that dramatic impact of automation was conspicuous by its absence but that in the future major changes in organizational structure may be expected as the automation of decision making occurs. Banks have now instituted changes in organizational structure that would not have been possible without computerized systems, but the automation of decision making has not occurred, at least not for the typical managerial decision. Instead, there has been computerization of information files and techniques for modeling future trends in so-called decision support systems. It is possible that we are now at the same stage with respect to use of computer databases that Yavitz observed with respect to use of computers some sixteen years ago.

The study by Vaughan and Porat, *Banking Computer Style* (1969), concluded that within given banks some changes were taking place because of more information available at faster speeds. However, the changes were subtle and difficult to categorize. About the most that could be said was that changes in the information systems would occur much more quickly than related structural changes in the organization. In international banking, there is definitely more information available faster, not only because of advanced telecommunications and computer systems among banks, but also because of increased cooperation among central banks and regulatory agencies and the increased information gathering by the regulatory agencies.

Generally, large banks have been in line with other large businesses in the attempt to automate the office and to make use of the most current information processing technology. To be more accurate, the largest commercial banks seem to be among the leaders in developing information technology. The institutional decentralization proposed by the 1973 OECD study, *Automated Information Management in Public Administration*, as a development not yet evident in public administration, can be observed in international banking, where foreign branches or offices have developed substantial independence within decentralized managements.

The organizational issue is particularly pertinent to this interorganization study because of the suspicion at the outset that the network of interorganization relations was beginning to resemble an organization itself and that, simultaneously, organizations themselves were changing. In international banking, there exists a set of people who are able to communicate and willing to contribute action for a common purpose. But the common purpose needs qualification. Although there is general cooperation among central banks for the common purpose of stabilizing the world economy, it is not accurate to describe the relations among central banks as a single organization. Each central bank owes allegiance to its own country. Among commercial banks, there is often cooperative action for a common purpose in the syndication of loans or in consortia banking, but syndicated loans represent only temporary arrangements for very specific ends. Therefore, only in the most general terms can a common purpose be ascribed to the interbank relationships.

Counter to that though, in international banking there are indicators of the "future organization" discussed in chapter 1. There are, for example, computerized arrangements for information processing and transfer among fairly independent units. There is coordination among the units on a fairly direct basis. There is no clear unity of command. There are multiauthority relationships and a central pool of planners coexisting with the relatively independent units. What does not seem apparent yet is that the large commercial banks share the same computerized information held in economic databases.

As perhaps partial support for the notion that the large international banks are as a group prefiguring the organization of the future, a recent study related computer/telecommunications to a federated form of organization. The forecast by the Center for Futures Research at the University of Southern California concludes that telecommunications might create a climate where groups bound by interests and not geography can form (for example, in banking), exhibiting diversity and pluralism in a federated approach.[7] But the forecast also notes that values and beliefs may hinder this. For example, people may think that computer systems depersonalize their lives and make it more difficult to control one's own environment. The computer systems, then, might be feared, resented, and opposed. The concerns over privacy of personal data in computerized databases has been one area where opposition has been apparent.

As the early banking automation studies were pretty much forced to conclude, the dramatic evidence of technology-related changes is absent, but probably only because not enough time has elapsed for the gradual changes to take place.

Social Impact

The broader social environment of multinational, interorganization computer/telecommunications is one of steadily increasing interdependence and obvious desires for cooperative mutually beneficial systems. This is especially true for Western Europe, and particularly so since World War II, but it is also true for other industrialized countries, including the United States and Japan.

The cooperative efforts growing out of the transborder data flow debates indicate that leaders in a variety of countries are determined to work together, to harmonize their legislation regarding computer networks and to provide standards for increased exchanges. This seems apparent even though complete cooperation and mutual understanding does not exist, and international treaties and conventions face continuing objections from various interest groups. Rules of international law are expected sometime during the 1980s, especially in banking, in order to establish liability, for example, in international electronic fund transfers.[8] In the survey discussed in chapter 4, some 72 percent of all respondents agreed that the global aspect of problems is often more important than the viewpoint of any one nation.

Throughout the international debates regarding transborder computer networks a recurring theme is that information is a key resource and information processing is a key activity in modern society. Within the information economy, banking is becoming one of the prime segments. The nature of banking requires information about the world and massive storing and transmitting of information about accounts. Here again, however, it is necessary to look at specific areas of information gathering, processing, and transferring to understand what this means. Bankers rely a great deal on unstructured, informal information gathered through personal contacts (as do most managers). Computer systems have not affected this to any great degree. Computer databases are not used as the primary decision-making mechanism. The presence of computer networks is being felt, however, in information systems involving specific definable units that have long been elements of international trade. As a small example, the time for settlement among the New York Clearing House banks has been moved up three hours and will be moved up eventually to same-day settlement. This is a direct result of the use of CHIPS by international organizations. As another example, Fed Wire may eventually use one set of national operating hours rather than several sets of regional operating hours as at present. This will mean that some banks may have to change the working day of some of their employees, either to begin earlier or to stay later to handle the activity on the network.

In a sense, there has been indirect homogenization of the way people understand and interpret problems, which was a forecast of the 1972 Delphi study reviewed in the first chapter. In international banking, central banks and bank regulatory agencies work together to share ideas about the problems of multinational banking. Often, the increased international presence of banks has resulted in mutual appreciation of another country's banking and financial practices. Most of the forecasts of that study, in fact, appear to have been accurate. For example, international computer networks have fostered greater integration of an organization's activities and, at the same time, less centralized and less hierarchical management structures. The one forecast that does not seem to have been borne out by time was the suggestion that there would be little if any movement in the direction of uniformity of relevant national laws. In Western Europe, the Council of Europe, the OECD, and especially the European Community have been engaged in considerable effort for just that end.

Whether or not computerized information processing networks are contributing directly to more societywide planning is a difficult question. In some situations, there are indications that banks, as a group, are exerting demonstrable influence in world affairs. As a senior vice-president at Manufacturers Hanover Trust has written in regard to syndicated loans, the principle bankers of a given country can collectively exert persuasive pressure at crucial times.[9] Others have argued that banks, in making large loans to national governments, are actually engaged in foreign aid and are making foreign policy decisions.[10] As this study has attempted to demonstrate, the actual state of affairs is much more complex than these statements indicate. As a point of interest, in the survey summarized in chapter 4, only 15 percent of the respondents disagreed with the statement that the major international banks work together to stabilize the world economy, although another 27 percent were uncertain one way or the other.

Limitations and Suggestions

This study of interorganization relations and information processing networks chose the case of international banking because of its status as a leading area of advanced information technology. The disadvantage of choosing banking is that it is unique in many ways as an information processing industry. However, in the context of the information-based society, the information processing developments in banking have value for other segments of society. Thus the organizational and social effects associated with information processing itself should be broadly relevant.

There are some industries other than banking that have international computer networks and that engage in a good deal of interaction. These industries probably do not exhibit the same degree of interorganization relations as in international banking, but they might be additional candidates nonetheless for an investigation of the effects of the use of information processing networks. The airlines industry has an international computer and teletype network linking twenty computer systems and several hundred airlines. The twenty distinct computer systems, operated by different airlines, in turn serve other airlines; thus, groups of airline organizations are subject to the formalization and standardization of message traffic that accompanies use of a computer system. The oil industry is probably another candidate for an analysis of interorganization information processing, and a third possibility is in the emergence of worldwide credit card systems.

The survey portion of this study was conducted with a number of restraints. The survey only addressed conditions among the largest commercial banks, since computerization historically developed within the larger organizations first. And the survey was aimed only at officers who might report the greatest amount of telecommunications use, the greatest amount of database use, and the greatest amount of computer network use, since the intent of the survey was to measure the maximum extent of the current situation of electronic exchanges. Admittedly other departments of banking organizations would have reported less computer/telecommunications interaction. Also, the survey findings are the results of personal estimates or perceptions on the part of the respondents. Corroborating evidence, where available, seems to indicate that these were informed estimates, but it is not known how many of the responses were based on available internal statistics and how many were based on 'best guesses.'

The breadth of this study, although international, was limited primarily to Western Europe, North America, and Japan, because these are the nations most involved in collective efforts in international banking. Other regions of the world have their own collaborative or cooperative arrangements in banking, but their banks are not, with few exceptions, among the fifty largest. Examples of national developments were restricted to the United States because the literature is extensive and because it is most readily available to a researcher in the United States. This does not mean that the United States is the most advanced country in computerized banking. It is not. Nor is the United States the most open country to international efforts at harmonization of relevant legislation; in fact, the United States seems to have pursued a policy of delaying efforts at harmonization.

Further research might focus on other geographic areas, perhaps specifically on Western Europe, where there have been continuing, encompassing efforts toward a true community. Other research might be directed at banks (or other corporations) in the newly industrialized countries and in other third world countries, where regionalism is also said to be replacing strict nationalism.

Organizationally, one of the key areas needing more attention is the test of organization-behavior theories on the cluster organization. Do theories of organization behavior involving personality, motivation, leadership, participative management, change, or communication apply as well to the multinational cluster organization as to individual organizations? Further studies are needed to test the notion that there are indeed cluster organizations based on computerized information processing networks.

The present study does not try to prove, as if in a chemistry experiment, the existence of a supraorganization or cluster organization associated with computerized information processing systems. As Barzun and Graff have stated, any attempt to distinguish the paramount cause of some human development is foolishly misleading.[11] The historical researcher tries to understand and describe a chain of events, but it is open to the researcher's insight to select the events and up to the audience to judge the usefulness of the effort as a means of organizing facts. It is the assumptions and judgments of researchers that eventually comprise our knowledge of organizations.

Regarding banking organizations particularly, others have argued that we do not yet appreciate the full impact of technology on society and the impact of the political environment on technological development.[12] The transborder data flow debates, for example, should be recognized as a prime political aspect of the telecommunications interaction among banks, even though banks' networks have thus far been exempt from existing legislation affecting international traffic in personal data. As for the impact of technology, there are indications that the international networks for information processing are having a visible effect, as outlined on the previous pages and as mentioned in the studies of others. For example, in Western Europe the Eurocheque Card System is a system developed by four countries and accepted by 20,000 banks in about forty countries. The card itself is not only a check guarantee card but also a means of making purchases in the local currency of one country using a card issued in another country.[13] Another suggested outcome is the emergence of superbanks, that is, a few giant organizations dominating the world financial markets.[14]

The value of the suggestions in the present study is in their usefulness as a means of organizing knowledge about the world. If, as time passes, the descriptions of the collegial form of supraorganization or cluster organization seem to be accurate, and to be generalizable to other groups of organizations, then we may have a means of understanding some of the ways technology affects society and society molds technology. If it happens that organizations of the future do not exhibit the characteristics of the cluster organization, or if the characteristics are not particularly insightful, then clearly the usefulness of the concept is much in doubt. So far, on the basis of our present knowledge of organizations and of the interplay between technology and society, the cluster organization concept appears to represent reality.

Conclusion

The purpose of this analysis was to describe and explain the patterns and developments in international banking related to the use of computerized information processing networks. The result is an indication that, in international banking, such networks have strengthened existing telecommunications patterns while providing the means for somewhat more facile and more coordinated inter-organization exchanges and information transfers. The situation approaches a form of cluster organization—built on the past, yet different again.

Moreover, there are numerous indications that, internationally, values and beliefs favor cooperative ventures, especially on the regional level if not globally. When Thomas Whisler wrote that the ultimate shape of technology is an inkblot to us, that we see what we want to see, he nevertheless went on to "see" structure in the inkblot. He saw the loose organization of the future, the cluster organization, held together by information processing technology. The inter-organization relations analyzed on the preceding pages appear to be changing in the way Whisler supposed.

Notes

1. Herbert A. Simon, "Decision Making and Organizational Design," in *Organization Theory*, ed. D.S. Pugh (New York: Penguin Books, 1971), p. 206.

2. Karlene H. Roberts, Charles L. Hulin, and Denise M. Rousseau, *Developing an Interdisciplinary Science of Organizations* (San Francisco: Jossey-Bass, 1978), p. 25.

3. Howard Aldrich, *Organizations and Environments* (Englewood Cliffs, N.J.: Prentice-Hall, 1979), p. xi.

4. See, for example, Cameron Rondo, Olga Crisp, Hugh T. Patrick, and Richard Tilly, *Banking in the Early Stages of Industrialization* (New York: Oxford University Press, 1967).

5. Ian Morrison and Dimitri Vittas, "The Structure of Banking Systems Abroad," *Bank Administration* 55 (October 1979): 49-53.

6. P. Henry Mueller, "A Conspectus for Offshore Lenders," in *Offshore Lending by U.S. Commercial Banks*, ed. F. John Mathis (Washington, D.C.: Bankers' Association for Foreign Trade, 1975), pp. 12-13.

7. Herbert S. Dordick, Helen G. Bradley, Burt Nanus, and Thomas H. Martin, "Network Information Services—The Emergence of an Industry," *Journal of Telecommunications Policy* 3 (September 1979): 217-234.

8. Ithiel de Sola Pool and Richard J. Solomon, "The Regulation of Trans-border Data Flows," *Telecommunications Policy* 3 (September 1979): 176-191.

9. James R. Greene, "Financing Foreign Governments and Official Entities," in *Offshore Lending*, ed. Mathis, p. 200.

10. See, for example, Jack Zwick and Richard K. Goeltz, "U.S. Banks Are Making Foreign Policy," *New York Times*, 18 March 1979, p. F14.

11. Jacques Barzun and Henry F. Graff, *The Modern Researcher* (New York: Harcourt, Brace and World, 1970), pp. 171-172.

12. John Leslie King and Kenneth L. Kraemer, "Electronic Funds Transfer as a Subject of Study in Technology, Society and Public Policy," in *Computers and Banking*, ed. K. Colton and K. Kraemer (New York: Plenum Press, 1980), pp. 169-181.

13. Thomas F. Horan, "Outlook for EFT Technology," in *Computers and Banking*, ed. Colton and Kraemer, pp. 21-38.

14. Rob Kling, "The Social and Institutional Meanings of Electronic Funds Transfer Systems," in *Computers and Banking*, ed. Colton and Kraemer, pp. 183-195.

Bibliography

"ABA Surveying Bank Voice, Data Transmissions." *American Banker*, 20 February 1979, p. 2.

Abelson, Philip H., and Hammond, Allen L. "The Electronics Revolution." *Science* 195 (18 March 1977): 1087-1092.

Aldom, Robert S.; Purdy, Alan B; Schneider, Robert T.; and Whittingham, Harry E., Jr. *Automation in Banking*. New Brunswick, N.J.: Rutgers University Press, 1963.

Aldrich, Howard. "An Interorganization Dependency Perspective on Relations between the Employment Service and Its Organization Set." In *The Management of Organization Design*, edited by Ralph H. Kilman, Louis R. Pondy, and Dennis P. Slevin. Amsterdam: North-Holland Publishing Co., 1976.

Aldrich, Howard E. *Organizations and Environments*. Englewood Cliffs, N.J.: Prentice-Hall, 1979.

Aliber, Robert Z. "Towards a Theory of International Banking." *Federal Reserve Bank of San Francisco Economic Review*, Spring 1976, pp. 5-8.

Anderla, Georges. *Information in 1985*. Paris: Organization for Economic Cooperation and Development, 1973.

Anderson, Ronald. "Automation and the Cashless-Checkless Society." In *The Impact of the Computer on Commercial Banking*, edited by F. Fabozzi. Hempstead, N.Y.: Hofstra University, 1975.

Arenson, Karen W. "A Battered Euromarket Thrives." *New York Times*, 3 February 1980, sect. 12, p. 23.

Argyris, Chris. *Organization of a Bank*. New Haven, Conn.: Yale University Labor and Management Center, 1974.

"Arnold Toynbee: Are Businessmen Creating the Pax Romana?" Interview. *Forbes*, 11 April 1974, pp. 68-70.

Baker, James C., and Bradford, M. Gerald. *American Banks Abroad*. New York: Praeger Publishers, 1974.

Balderston, F.E.; Carman, James M.; and Hoggatt, Austin C. "Computers in Banking and Marketing." *Science* 195 (18 March 1977): 1115-1119.

Bank for International Settlements. *Eight European Central Banks*. New York: Frederick A. Praeger, Publisher, 1963.

Barnard, Chester. *The Functions of the Executive*. Cambridge, Mass.: Harvard University Press, 1938.

Bell, Daniel. *The Coming of Post-Industrial Society*. New York: Basic Books, 1973.

_____. "Teletext and Technology." *Encounter*, June 1977, pp. 9-29.

_____. "Communications Technology—For Better or for Worse." *Harvard Business Review* 57 (May-June 1979): 20-42.

Bender, Mark G. *EFTS. Electronic Funds Transfer Systems.* Port Washington, N.Y.: Kennikat Press, 1975.

Benson, J. Kenneth. "The Interorganizational Network as a Political Economy." *Administrative Science Quarterly* 20 (June 1975): 229-249.

Bernasconi, F.A. "Informatics Integral to a New International Economic and Information Order." *Data Regulation. European and Third World Realities.* Uxbridge: Online Conferences, 1978.

Boulding, Kenneth E. "The Future of the Interaction of Knowledge, Energy and Materials." *Behavior Science Research* 13 (1978): 169-183.

Brandt, William K., and Hulbert, James M. "Patterns of Communications in the Multinational Corporation: An Empirical Study." *Journal of International Business Studies* 7 (Spring 1976): 57-64.

Branscomb, Lewis M. "Information: The Ultimate Frontier." *Science* 203 (January 1979): 143-147.

Burnham, David. "U.S. Is Worried by World Efforts to Curtail Flow of Information." *New York Times,* 26 February 1978, p. 1.

Bush, Vannevar. "As We May Think." *Atlantic Monthly*, July 1945, pp. 101-108.

Calleo, David P., ed. *Money and the Coming World Order.* New York: New York University Press, 1976.

Cameron, Rondo; Crisp, Olga; Patrick, Hugh T.; and Tilly, Richard. *Banking in the Early Stages of Industrialization.* New York: Oxford University Press, 1967.

Carbaugh, Robert J., and Fan Liang-Shing. *The International Monetary System.* Lawrence, Kans.: University Press of Kansas, 1976.

Carmody, Frank. "The Work of the European Community in the Area of Computers and Privacy." *Data Regulation. European and Third World Realities.* Uxbridge: Online Conferences, 1978.

Center for Medieval and Renaissance Studies, University of California, Los Angeles. *The Dawn of Modern Banking.* New Haven, Conn.: Yale University Press, 1979.

"Citibank Seeks Productivity in Corporate Service Sector." *Bank Systems and Equipment,* July 1978, pp. 38-39.

Clark, Lindley H., Jr. "U.S. Monetary Troubles." *Wall Street Journal,* 13 October 1978, p. 22.

Cleveland, Harlan. "Interdependence: Where You Stand Depends on Where You Sit." *California Management Review* 20 (Fall 1977): 93-96.

Colton, Kent W., and Kraemer, Kenneth L., eds. *Computers and Banking.* New York: Plenum Press, 1980.

Cuadra Associates. *Directory of Non-Bibliographic Database Services.* Draft edition. Santa Monica, Calif.: Cuadra Associates, 1979.

Darrath, Owen K. "New Body Urged for Regulation of Data Flow." *Computerworld*, 27 February 1978, p. 9.

Directory of Computer Based Services. Vienna, Virg.: Telenet Communications Corporation, 1979.

Deutsch, Karl W. "Knowledge in the Growth of Civilization: A Cybernetic Approach to the History of Human Thought." In *The Foundations of Access to Knowledge,* edited by Edward B. Montgomery. Syracuse, N.Y.: Syracuse University Press, 1968.

Dordick, Herbert S.; Bradley, Helen G.; Nanus, Burt; and Martin, Thomas H. "Network Information Services—The Emergence of an Industry." *Journal of Telecommunications Policy* 3 (September 1979): 217-234.

"DP Costs Rising 12 Per Cent." *Bank Systems and Equipment,* November 1978, p. 66.

EFT in the United States. The Final Report of the National Commission on Electronic Fund Transfers. Washington, D.C.: U.S. Government Printing Office, 1977.

Eger, John. "Transborder Data Flow." *Datamation,* November 1978, pp. 50-54.

———. "U.S. Proposals for Progress through Negotiations." *Journal of Communication* 29 (Summer 1979): 124-128.

Ellington, William. "U.S. Banks Are Losing Their Dominance in Eurocurrency Lending, Figures Show." *Wall Street Journal,* 14 December 1978, p. 18.

Emery, James C. "Managerial and Economic Issues in Distributed Computing." In *Information Processing 77: Proceedings of the IFIP Congress 1977,* edited by Bruce Gilchrist. Amsterdam: North-Holland Publishing Company, 1977, pp. 945-955.

Fabozzi, Frank J., ed. *The Impact of the Computer on Commercial Banking.* Hofstra University Yearbook of Business, series 11, vol. 2. Hempstead, N.Y.: Hofstra University, 1975.

Farnsworth, Clyde H. "The New Multinationals." *New York Times,* 4 March 1979, p. F13.

"Fed Seeks Comment on Free Trade Zone for New York City." *Wall Street Journal,* 15 December 1978, p. 13.

Fishman, William L. "International Data Flow: Personal Privacy and Some Other Issues." Paper presented at the Fourth International Conference on Computer Communication, Kyoto, Japan, September 1978.

"The Fifty Largest Commercial Banking Companies." *Fortune,* July 1978, pp. 116-117.

"Foreign Banks in London." *The Banker,* November 1978, pp. 65-129.

"Foreign Banks Unlikely to Exert Undue Control in U.S. Market, PSI Study Says." *American Banker,* 3 November 1979, pp. 2, 7.

"Foreign Loans by Banks Grew in First Half." *Wall Street Journal,* 8 December 1978, p. 37.

Forest, Robert B. "Close Cooperation: Europe's Best Hope." *Datamation,* 15 December 1971, pp. 26-28.

"The Fortune Directory of the Fifty Largest Commercial Banking Companies Outside the U.S." *Fortune,* 13 August 1979, pp. 206-207.

Foy, Nancy. "Computer Policy for the Common Market." *Datamation*, June 1973, pp. 139, 152.

Frank, Ronald A. "Eger Warns Privacy Laws Blocking Data Flow." *Computerworld*, 20 March 1978, p. 21.

French, Nancy. "U.S. 'Wins' at Data Flow Parley." *Computerworld*, 3 October 1977, pp. 1, 4.

Galbraith, John Kenneth. *The New Industrial State.* Boston: Houghton Mifflin Company, 1971.

Ganley, Oswald H. "International Data Flows: Shall We Have International Competition?" Paper presented at the University of Washington Conference on Communications, Seattle, 12 December 1977.

_____. "The Role of Communications and Information Resources in Canada." Harvard University, Program on Information Resources Policy, Cambridge, Massachusetts, 1979.

_____. "Transborder Data Flow–A Significant Factor in World Trade?" Paper presented at the Second Annual Conference on Transborder Data Flows, Washington, D.C.. 18 June 1979.

_____. "Transborder Data Flow–On beyond Privacy." Paper prepared for the Harvard University Program on Information Resources Policy, Cambridge, Massachusetts, undated.

Garvey, George, and Blyn, Martin R. *The Velocity of Money.* New York: Federal Reserve Bank of New York, 1969.

Gassmann, H.P. "The Activities of OECD in the Field of Transnational Data Regulation." *Data Regulation. European and Third World Realities.* Uxbridge: Online Conferences, 1978.

_____. "Data Networks: A New Information Infrastructure." *OECD Observer*, no. 95 (November 1978), pp. 10-16.

Gesellschaft fur Mathematik und Datenverarbeitung, l'Institute de Recherche d'Informatique et d'Automatique, and the National Computing Centre. "Joint Study on Data Security and Confidentiality. Interim Report." April 1979.

"A Global Processing Network." *Datamation*, September 1978, p. 154.

Gotlieb, Allan; Dalfen, Charles; and Katz, Kenneth. "The Transborder Transfer of Information by Communications and Computer Systems; Issues and Approaches to Guiding Principles." *American Journal of International Law* 68 (April 1974): 227-257.

Haas, Ernst B. *The Web of Interdependence.* Englewood Cliffs, N.J.: Prentice-Hall, 1970.

Hall, Richard H. *Organizations: Structure and Process.* Englewood Cliffs, N.J.: Prentice-Hall, 1977.

Hall, Robert A. "Where EFT in Wholesale Banking Stands Today, and Where It's Going." *Banking,* May 1978, pp. 45-48.

Hamelink, Cees J. "Informatics: Third World Call for New Order." *Journal of Communication* 29 (Summer 1979): 144-148.

Hasenyager, Bruce W. "Automating the Office." *ACM Proceedings 1978*. New York: ACM, 1978, pp. 190-191.

Heenan, David A., and Keegan, Warren J. "The Rise of the Third World Multinationals." *Harvard Business Review* 57 (January-February 1979): 101-109.

Heilprin, L.B. "On the Information Problem Ahead." *American Documentation* 12 (January 1961): 6-14.

"Heimann Calls the Shots for Overseas Lending." *The Economist*, 14 January 1978, pp. 99-100.

Hochmuth, Milton S. *Organizing the Transnational*. Leiden: A.W. Sijthoff, 1974.

Holmes, Edith. "U.S. Stand on Data Flow Seen Months Away." *Computerworld*, 6 February 1978, p. 10.

_____. "French Commit Funds to Develop Database Industry." *Information World*, August 1979, pp. 1, 17.

Hondius, Frits. "Council of Europe Nearing Completion of Treaty on International Data Protection and Privacy." *Computerworld*, 21 January 1980, pp. 18-19.

Hondius, F.W. "The Work of the Council of Europe in the Area of Data Protection." *Data Regulation. European and Third World Realities*. Uxbridge: Online Conferences, 1978.

Hu, Y.S. *The Impact of U.S. Investment in Europe*. New York: Praeger Publishers, 1973.

Humphreys, Arthur L.C. "The British/Western European Viewpoint." In *Expanding Use of Computers in the 70s*, edited by Fred Gruenberger. Englewood Cliffs, N.J.: Prentice-Hall, 1971.

Hyman, Joan Prevette. "Bank Wire II Is Seen as Good Backup to Fed Wire; Scores Points on Services." *Bank Systems and Equipment*, September 1978, pp. 72-76.

"IDC Cuts Databases Down to Size to Boost Revenues and Usefulness." *Online Database Report*, June 1979, p. 1.

"Information as Fundamental as Energy—Harvard University Program." *Information World*, May 1979, p. 16.

"Information Sector Growth." *Information World*, March 1979, p. 17.

"International Banking." *Federal Reserve Bank of San Francisco Economic Review*, Spring 1976, pp. 3-4.

"International Barriers to Data Flows." Report prepared for the use of the Committee on Interstate and Foreign Commerce of the House of Representatives. 96th Cong. 1st sess., April 1979. Washington, D.C.: U.S. Government Printing Office, 1979.

Jacobson, Robert E. "The Hidden Issues: What Kind of Order?" *Journal of Communication* 29 (Summer 1979): 149-155.

Janssen, Richard F. "World-wide Foreign Exchange Volume Is Placed Roughly at $50 Trillion a Year." *Wall Street Journal*, 15 January 1979, p. 7.

Kaplan, Arnold, and Lange, Per. "Highlights from the '79 Bank Telecommunications Survey." *ABA Banking Journal*, February 1980, pp. 92-95.

Katz, Daniel, and Kahn, Robert L. *The Social Psychology of Organizations.* New York: John Wiley and Sons, 1966.

Kirchner, Jake. "OECD's Data Protection Guidelines Near Finish." *Computerworld*, 19 March 1979, p. 10.

_____. "OECD Meets in Paris to Head Off Piecemeal Data Flow Legislation." *Computerworld*, 15 October 1979, p. 3.

_____. "'Legitimate Concerns' Seen Behind Data Protection Laws." *Computerworld*, 12 November 1979, p. 34.

Klopstock, Fred H. "Foreign Banks in the United States: Scope and Growth of Operations." Federal Reserve Bank of New York, Research Paper no. 7316, 1973.

Kroloff, George, and Cohen, Scott. "The New World Information Order." Report prepared for the Committee on Foreign Relations of the U.S. Senate, November 1977.

Kutler, Jeffrey. "Word Processing Technology Ahead of Most Banks' Abilities to Use It." *American Banker*, 3 January 1979, p. 8.

_____. "Ultimate Growth of Home Banking Awaits Resolution of Legal, Technical Issues." *American Banker*, 24 January 1979, pp. 8-9.

_____. "Spread of Transborder Data Flow Laws Compounds Intl Operations Challenge." *American Banker*, 7 March 1979, p. 12.

_____. "SWIFT Codifies Liabilities." *American Banker*, 18 June 1979, pp. 1, 22.

_____. "FDIC Finds EFT Has Not Meant Big Bank Domination." *American Banker,* 30 October 1979, pp. 1, 22.

_____. "Fed May Link Transfer Net." *American Banker*, 16 November 1979, pp. 1, 5.

_____. "Through Acquisition, Citibank NA Becomes Developer and Vendor of Office Automation." *American Banker*, 21 November 1979, pp. 6-7.

Leavitt, Harold; Pinfield, Lawrence; and Webb, Eugene, eds. *Organizations of the Future.* New York: Praeger Publishers, 1974.

Lees, Francis A. *Foreign Banking and Investment in the United States.* New York: John Wiley and Sons, 1976.

Lewin, Wayne B., and Taylor, David van L. "CHIPS, An Evolving Electronic Funds Transfer System." *Bank Administration* 55 (November 1979): 36-39.

Lewis, Paul. "Europe's Currency Ties to Start." *New York Times*, 13 March 1979, p. D1.

_____. "A New Monetarism Sweeps the West." International Economic Survey Section, *New York Times*, 3 February 1980, p. 14.

Lindberg, Leon N., ed. *Politics and the Future of Industrial Society.* New York: David McKay Company, 1976.

Lundell, E. Drake, Jr. "Criticism of IBM Muted but Evident at Meeting." *Computerworld*, 11 September 1978, p. 6.

_____. "Infighting between Sponsors Mars Conference." *Computerworld*, 11 September 1978, p. 5.

_____. "SPIN Nations Hammer Out Details of New World Order." *Computerworld*, 11 September 1978, pp. 1, 4.

Machlup, Fritz. *The Production and Distribution of Knowledge in the United States*. Princeton, N.J.: Princeton University Press, 1962.

McPherson, John R. "Electronic Mail: It's Here Today." *Banking*, March 1978, pp. 16, 19.

March, James G., and Simon, Herbert A. *Organizations*. New York: John Wiley and Sons, 1958.

Mariolis, Peter. "Interlocking Directorates and Control of Corporations: The Theory of Bank Control." *Social Science Quarterly* 56 (December 1975): 425-439.

Marrett, Cora Bagley. "On the Specification of Interorganizational Dimensions." *Sociology and Social Research* 56 (October 1971): 83-99.

Martyn, Howe. *Multinational Business Management*. Lexington, Mass.: Lexington Books, D.C. Heath, 1970.

Masmoudi, Mustapha. "The New World Information Order." *Journal of Communication* 29 (Spring 1979): 172-185.

Masuda, Yoneji. "Privacy in the Future Information Society." *Computer Networks* 3 (June 1979): 164-170.

Mathis, F. John, ed. *Offshore Lending by U.S. Commercial Banks*. Washington, D.C.: Bankers' Association for Foreign Trade, 1975.

Mayer, Martin. *The Bankers*. New York: Weybright and Talley, 1974.

Meadows, Edward. "How the Euromarket Fends Off Global Financial Disaster." *Fortune*, 24 September 1979, pp. 122-135.

Mills, C. Wright. *The Power Elite*. New York: Oxford University Press, 1959.

Mitchell, H.F., Jr. "The Future of the Switching Computer." *Datamation*, February 1965, pp. 24-25.

Moody's Bank and Finance Manual, vol. 1. New York: Moody's Investors Service, 1978.

Morison, Ian, and Vittas, Dimitri. "The Structure of Banking Systems Abroad." *Bank Administration* 55 (October 1979): 49-53.

Moskowitz, Warren E. "Global Asset and Liability Management at Commercial Banks." *Federal Reserve Bank of New York Quarterly Review* 4 (Spring 1979): 42-48.

Musgrave, William. "The Computerized Work Station." *Dun's Review*, July 1978, pp. 109-111.

Myers, Edith. "EFT: Despite Hurdles—Growth." *Datamation*, July 1978, pp. 187-188.

Nanus, Burt; Wooton, Michael; and Borko, Harold. "The Social Implications of the Use of Computers across National Boundaries." *AFIPS Conference Proceedings 1973.* Montvale, N.J.: AFIPS Press, 1973, pp. 735-745.

New York, State of. *Annual Report of the Superintendent of Banks.* Albany, N.Y.: New York State Banking Department, 1977.

"New York Banks Propose a 'Free Trade Zone' for Their International Business." *Wall Street Journal,* 30 November 1978, p. 1.

"The New Wild Blue Yonder of Bank Communications." *Banking,* May 1977, pp. 42-43, 82.

"Nonbibliographic Databases Online." *Online Review* 3 (June 1979): 153-174.

Nora, Simon, and Minc, Alain. *Report on the Computerization of Society. Introduction.* Paris: Board of Financial Examiners, 1978.

Nordenstreng, K., and Schiller, Herbert I. "Helsinki: The New Equation." *Journal of Communication* 26 (1976): 130-134.

Oettinger, Anthony G.; Berman, Paul J.; and Read, William H. *High and Low Politics; Information Resources for the 80s.* Cambridge, Mass.: Ballinger Publishing Company, 1977.

Organization for Economic Cooperation and Development. *Information for a Changing Society.* Paris: OECD, 1971.

_____. *Automated Information Management in Public Administration.* OECD Informatics Studies, vol. 4. Paris: OECD, 1973.

_____. *Conference on Computer/Telecommunication Policy.* OECD Informatics Studies, vol. 11. Paris: OECD, 1975.

_____. *Policy Issues in Data Protection and Privacy.* OECD Informatics Studies, vol. 10. Paris: OECD, 1976.

_____. *The Usage of International Data Networks in Europe.* Paris: OECD, 1979.

Pantages, Angeline. "Canada's Economic Concerns." *Datamation,* 1 November 1978, pp. 67-75.

_____. "Europe Moves toward Controlled Data Flow." *Datamation,* 1 November 1978, pp. 80-82.

Penniman, D.; Butrimenko, A.; and Page, J. "International Data Exchange and the Application of Informatics Technology." Paper prepared for the International Institute for Applied Systems Analysis, Schloss Laxenburg, Austria, December 1977.

Perrow, Charles. "A Framework for the Comparative Analysis of Organizations." *American Sociological Review* 32 (April 1967): 194-208.

Peters, Richard A., and Simpson, Keppel M. "Eurodata: Data Communications in Europe 72-85." *Datamation,* December 1973, pp. 76-80.

Pfeffer, Jeffrey, and Leblebici, Huseyin. "Information Technology and Organizational Structure." *Pacific Sociological Review* 20 (April 1977): 241-262.

Pfeffer, Jeffrey, and Salancik, Gerald R. *The External Control of Organizations.* New York: Harper and Row, 1978.

Pipe, G. Russell. "Australians Favor International Privacy Accord." *Computerworld,* 7 November 1977, pp. 17, 22.

_____. "International Treaty on Data Protection, Privacy in Limbo." *Computerworld,* 28 January 1980, pp. 20-21, 25.

_____. "National Policies, International Debates." *Journal of Communication* 29 (Summer 1979): 114-122.

_____. "Council of Europe Data Privacy Draft Delayed." *Computerworld,* 12 February 1979, p. 21.

Polk's World Bank Directory. Nashville, Tenn.: R.L. Polk and Company, 1978.

Pool, Ithiel de Sola, ed. *The Social Impact of the Telephone.* Cambridge, Mass.: MIT Press, 1977.

Pool, Ithiel de Sola, and Solomon, Richard J. "The Regulation of Transborder Data Flows." *Telecommunications Policy,* September 1979, pp. 176-191.

Porat, Marc U. "Defining an Information Sector in the U.S. Economy." *Information Reports and Bibliographies* 5: 17-31.

Porat, Marc Uri. *The Information Economy: Definition and Measurement.* A report prepared by the U.S. Department of Commerce, Office of Telecommunications. Washington, D.C.: U.S. Government Printing Office, 1977.

"Porat Urges More Research." *Information World,* March 1979, pp. 1, 18.

Presthus, Robert. *The Organizational Society.* New York: St. Martin's Press, 1978.

Price, James L. *Handbook of Organizational Measurement.* Lexington, Mass.: Lexington Books, D.C. Heath, 1972.

Ramström, Dick. "Toward an Information-Saturated Society." In *Organizations of the Future,* edited by Harold Leavitt, Lawrence Pinfield, and Eugene Webb. New York: Praeger Publishers, 1974.

Richman, Allan. "8 of 10 Banks/Thrifts Will Use Distributed Systems Eventually." *Bank Systems and Equipment,* July 1978, pp. 32-37.

Roberts, Karlene H.; Hulin, Charles L.; and Rousseau, Denise M. *Developing an Interdisciplinary Science of Organizations.* San Francisco: Jossey-Bass, 1978.

Robinson, Peter. "Transborder Dataflow—A Canadian Perspective." *Information Privacy* 2 (March 1980): 55-60.

Robinson, Stuart, Jr. *Multinational Banking.* Leiden: A.W. Sijthoff, 1972.

Rosenberg, Jerry M. *The Death of Privacy.* New York: Random House, 1969.

Rout, Lawrence. "Bank Invasion. Many Foreign Lenders Set Up Branches Here." *Wall Street Journal,* 24 November 1978, pp. 1, 25.

Rowthorn, Robert. *International Big Business 1957-1967.* Cambridge: Cambridge University Press, 1971.

Salera, Virgil. *Multinational Business.* Boston: Houghton Mifflin Co., 1969.

Saur, Ricardo A.C. "Protection without Protectionism." *Journal of Communication* 29 (Summer 1979): 138-140.

Scannell, Tim. "Lecht Voices Fears for Users' Survival in the 1980s." *Computerworld*, 11 June 1979, p. 7.

Serwatynski, William. "Transborder Dataflow—Lifeblood of Multinationals." *Information Privacy* 1 (November 1978): 81-86.

_____. "Transborder Dataflow: A Global View." *Information Privacy* 1 (January 1979): 133-136.

Short, Genie Dudding, and White, Betsy Buttrill. "International Bank Lending: A Guided Tour throuh the Data." *Federal Reserve Bank of New York Quarterly Review,* Autumn 1978, pp. 39-46.

Simon, Herbert A. *Administrative Behavior.* New York: The Macmillan Company, 1945.

_____. *The New Science of Management Decision.* Englewood Cliffs, N.J.: Prentice-Hall, 1977.

"Slow Start, but SWIFT Comeback." *Bank Systems and Equipment*, September 1978, p. 75.

Society for Worldwide Interbank Financial Telecommunication. *General Information*. Brussels, January 1978.

Sood, James H. "Personal Privacy: Can the MNCs Afford to Respect It?" *Columbia Journal of World Business* 14 (Spring 1979): 42-51.

Stern, Robert N. "The Development of an Interorganizational Control Network: The Case of Intercollegiate Athletics." *Administrative Science Quarterly* 24 (June 1979): 242-266.

"Study Finds Big Datacomm Advantage at Largest Banks." *American Banker*, 26 July 1978, p. 6.

"Sweden Regulates Those Snooping Data Banks." *Business Week*, 6 October 1973, pp. 93-95.

Szalai, Alexander. "The Future of International Organizations." In *Organizations of the Future*, edited by Harold Leavitt, Lawrence Pinfield, and Eugene Webb. New York: Praeger Publishers, 1974.

Thompson, James D. *Organizations in Action.* New York: McGraw-Hill Book Company, 1967.

Thoren, Margaret. "The Prime Mover at SWIFT: An Interview with Carl Reuterskiold." *Banker's Magazine,* September 1978, pp. 35-36.

Timberlake, Richard H., Jr. *Money, Banking, and Central Banking.* New York: Harper and Row, 1965.

Tomberg, Alex, ed. *Databases in Europe*. 3d edition. London: ASLIB, 1977.

"The Top 300." *The Banker*, June 1979, pp. 107-149.

"The Top 300 Banks." *World Banking 1978-79.* London: Investors Chronicle, 1979.

Touraine, Alain. *The Post-Industrial Society*, translated by Leonard F.X. Mayhew. New York: Random House, 1971.

Trolle-Schultz, Erik. "International Money Transfer Developments." *Journal of Bank Research* 9 (Summer 1978): 73-77.

Tuite, Matthew; Chisholm, Roger; and Radnor, Michael, eds. *Interorganizational Decision Making.* Chicago: Aldine Publishing Company, 1972.

Turk, Herman. "Interorganizational Networks in Urban Society: Initial Perspectives and Comparative Research." In *Social Networks*, edited by Samuel Leinhardt. New York: Academic Press, 1977.

Turn, Rein, comp. "Transborder Data Flow." *Computerworld,* 3 March 1980, pp. 60a-60j.

Turn, Rein, ed. *Transborder Data Flows.* Arlington, Virg.: American Federation of Information Processing Societies, 1979.

"The Two Worlds of Banking and EDP." *Datamation,* July 1965, p. 23.

U.S. Board of Governors of the Federal Reserve System. *Annual Report.* For all years, 1937-1979.

U.S. Comptroller of the Currency. *Annual Report.* For years 1975, 1976.

U.S. Congress. Senate. Committee on Foreign Relations. *Hearings before the Subcommittee on International Operations of the Committee on Foreign Relations.* 95th Cong., 1st sess., June 8-10, 1977. Washington, D.C.: U.S. Government Printing Office, 1977.

———. "The Role and Control of International Communications and Information." Report to the Subcommittee on International Operations of the Committee on Foreign Relations. 95th Cong., 1st sess., June 1977. Washington, D.C.: U.S. Government Printing Office, 1977.

U.S. Department of Health, Education and Welfare. Secretary's Advisory Committee on Automated Personal Data Systems. *Records, Computers and the Rights of Citizens.* Boston: Massachusetts Institute of Technology, 1973.

U.S. Domestic Council on the Right of Privacy. *National Information Policy.* Washington, D.C.: National Commission on Libraries and Information Science, 1976.

"U.S. Position: Guidelines vs. Treaty." *Datamation,* 1 November 1978, p. 81.

"The Use of Computers and Telecommunications. Towards an International Policy." *OECD Observer,* February 1973, pp. 17-28.

Uwe, Thomas. *Computerized Data Banks in Public Administration.* OECD Informatics Studies, vol. 1. Paris. OECD, 1971.

Vaughan, James A., and Porat, Avner M. *Banking Computer Style.* Englewood Cliffs, N.J.: Prentice-Hall, 1969.

Veith, Richard H. "Transborder Data Traffic: U.S. Unpredictability Is Unsettling." *Bulletin of the American Society for Information Science* 5 (August 1979): 24-25.

———. "Informatics and Transborder Data Flow: The Question of Social

Impact." *Journal of the American Society for Information Science* 31 (March 1980): 105-110.

_____. "Information Processing Networks in International Banking." *Social Science Information Studies*, forthcoming.

Vernon, Raymond. *Storm over the Multinationals*. Cambridge, Mass.: Harvard University Press, 1977.

Vernon, Raymond, ed. *Big Business and the State*. Cambridge, Mass.: Harvard University Press, 1974.

Westin, Alan F., dir., and Baker, Michael A. *Databanks in a Free Society*. Report of the Project on Computer Databanks of the Computer Science Board, National Academy of Sciences. New York: Quadrangle/The New York Times Book Co., 1972.

Westin, Alan F., ed. *Information Technology in a Democracy*. Cambridge, Mass.: Harvard University Press, 1971.

"What's Ahead for the Wire Services." *ABA Banking Journal*, February 1980, pp. 96-105.

Whetten, David A., and Leung, Thomas K. "The Instrumental Value of Inter-organizational Relations: Antecedents and Consequences of Linkage Formation." *Academy of Management Journal* 22 (June 1979): 325-344.

Whisler, Thomas. *The Impact of Computers on Organizations*. New York: Praeger Publishers, 1970.

_____. *Information Technology and Organizational Change*. Belmont, Calif.: Wadsworth Publishing Company, 1970.

_____. "The Business Organization of the Future." In *Organizations of the Future*, edited by Harold Leavitt, Lawrence Pinfield, and Eugene Webb. New York: Praeger Publishers, 1974.

"Why Telecommunications Has Become the Hot New Trend in Bank Operations." *Banking*, May 1977, pp. 90, 92.

Wilensky, Harold L. *Organizational Intelligence*. New York: Basic Books, 1967.

Wiseman, Toni. "Bank Terminals to Double by 1981: CSI." *Computerworld*, 3 October 1977, pp. 49-50.

Wren, Christopher S. "American Suggests News Pool to Cover 3rd World." *New York Times*, 9 April 1978, p. 5.

Wright, Pearce. "Facing a Booming Demand for Networks." *Datamation*, November 1973, pp. 138-139.

Wriston, Walter B. "The Euromarkets: Offspring of Technology." *American Banker*, 28 September 1979, pp. 16, 58.

Yavitz, Boris. *Automation in Banking. Its Process and Impact*. New York: The Graduate School of Business, Columbia University and the Free Press, 1967.

Index

Index

ABA. *See* American Banking Association
Aldom, Robert S., 37, 38, 106
Aldrich, Howard, 1, 8–9, 59–61, 104
Algemene Bank Nederland, 70, 73
American Banking Association, 36, 37–39
Amsterdam-Rotterdam Bank, 70, 73
Arbat Systems Ltd., 49
Argentina, 48, 94
Australia, 16–17, 20, 29, 30, 46, 94
Austria, xiii, 23, 29, 30, 48

Banca Commerciale Italiana, 70, 73
Banca Nazionale del Lavoro, 70, 73
Banco do Brasil, 71, 73
Bangkok, 44
Bank Administration Institute, 99
Bank for International Settlements, 98
Bank of America, 36, 40, 41, 42, 44, 51, 70, 74, 78
Bank of Canada, 52
Bank of England, 91, 96; statistical tables (database), 78
Bank of Montreal, 45, 70, 73
Bank of Nova Scotia, 71, 73
Bank of Tokyo, 70, 72, 74
Bank Wire, 47, 92
Bankers Trust Company, 8, 41, 42, 70, 71, 74
Banking, 1, 4–7, 11, 18, 35, 89–99; automation in, 36–41, 106–108; correspondent relationships, 53, 90, 92, 96; networks, 46–54
Banque Nationale de Paris, 70, 73
Barclays Bank, 70, 73
Barnard, Chester, 4
Barzun, Jacques, 111
Bayerische Landesbank Girozentrale, 71, 73
Bayerische Vereinsbank, 71, 73
Belgium, 48
Bell, Daniel, xiii, xiv–xv

Benin, 22
Benson, J. Kenneth, 6–7, 8–9
Bolivia, 22
Boston Clearing House, 89
Branscomb, Lewis, xi
Brazil, 29–30, 62, 72
Bush, Vannevar, xi

Caisse Nationale de Crédit Agricole, 71, 73
Canada, xiii, 16, 20, 23, 28–29, 30, 46, 47, 48, 62, 72, 79, 94
Canadian Imperial Bank of Commerce, 71, 73
Caploan, 78
Cash management programs, 39
Center for Futures Research, University of Southern California, 2–3, 107
Central banks, 91–92, 107, 109
Chartered Banks (database), 79
Chase Econometrics, 78, 79
Chase Manhattan Bank, 8, 40, 42, 70, 74
Chemical Bank, 8, 39, 70, 74
CHIPS. *See* Clearing House Interbank Payments System
Citibank, 8, 36, 40–41, 42, 50, 70, 74, 91, 105
Clearing House Interbank Payments System, 40, 47, 49, 53, 92–93, 109
Cluster organization, 5–6, 10–11, 105, 111, 112
Commerzbank, 70, 73
Comptroller of the Currency, 43, 45
Compustat Bankfile, 79
Computer networks, xi, xiv, xvi, 1–3, 10–11, 15–16, 17–19, 59, 66–68, 79, 80, 84, 87, 92–93, 94, 96–99, 103–112. *See also* Banking, networks
Continental Illinois Bank and Trust Company, 8, 41, 70, 74

About the Author

Richard H. Veith is currently a consultant with Logica Inc. working on international viewdata systems. He received a Ph.D. in information studies from Syracuse University, and an M.A. in radio and television from San Francisco State University. His previous publications include a book on two-way cable television in the United States, *Talk-Back TV: Two-Way Cable Television* (1976), and a dozen articles and conference papers on information technology and communications systems.